MIRROR OF OBSERVATION

A MIRROR THAT SEES EVERYTHING, UNDERSTANDS, THINKS AND WRITES ITS THOUGHTS ON IT.

BHARAT SHARMA

ISBN 979-888591022-4

Contents

Contents

Preface

"Atma Deepo Bhava"

This is an important thought of Buddha which means "be your lamp". Any person should take the purpose of his life or any moral and immoral decision himself. Taking every decision related to your life on your own and earning your useful knowledge yourself is called Atma Deepo Bhava.

This does not mean that you should not always take any advice or any knowledge from any other person by staying in an arrogant posture, it is not so, instead, you have to keep learning from everyone, which is the sign of a wise person. But Buddha wants to say here that with all those learned things, you have to use your mental power and in the end when the time of making any decision comes, then decide that decision from the thought woven by your mental power.

'I also, through this book, related my perspective, experience and my most special instrument, my "Mirror Of Observation" whose job is that whatever I see, I understand, I think and after that, I write my thoughts on it. The result of that is this book, in which there is no mention of only one issue, but every small and big aspect related to the life of all of us is included, from which we can learn anything well. It depends on you what kind of importance you give to which aspect of your life.

You to keep learning from this book, from every book in the world, from every person and environment around you through the priceless rule of Buddha and keep thinking while incorporating what you have learned into the decisions of your life.

Part One: The business talk that not everyone does.

The upper rules of doing business, you can also get by using your mobile internet data properly, but you need to know about some dark movements.

ONE

THE HIDDEN RULE OF BUSINESS :

The hidden rule of business :

Understand the concept of Perception + Make a Black list of your customers + know Your actual customers = Your business success with fewer disappointments.

Understand the concept of Perception

Having any kind of deficiency in a person is not so important as recognizing that deficiency at the right time, accepting it, without disturbing your ego, believing that I have this deficiency and I have to overcome it, So that the part of my life in which that lack is blocking my path so that I am not able to move forward in that part of life, I can move ahead by removing that shortcoming. I can develop myself in that part. But what if this positive thinking of yours does not get any support. By support, it means that you have never been able to recognize your lack and because of which you have to face constant disappointment in the part of your life in which you are constantly working hard. So in such a time of sorrow, only two paths can be found by an intelligent person.

First,

That person should recognize his deficiency and without shame and hurting his ego, remove that deficiency at the right time.

Second,

Someone who is justified in taking your friend's place, who will help you recognize your shortcomings, not to make fun of you in front of other people, Rather, its purpose should be to see you in the true sense without that drawback.

Based on this thinking, I want to be the "second" way of your life and especially your business or your future business. I want to play the role of that friend of yours, who genuinely wants to help you identify your shortcomings and the point is to remove that shortcoming, to make a decision about it, I have not yet become your best friend who deserves such a high level of authority over you. Therefore, in the end, after the search for that deficiency is completed, you will have to kill it with your own hands. Get ready to commit that good sin.

Now to walk on the path ahead, we have to borrow some words from a dictionary and we have to change those words according to our situation.

As in this question, what is your biggest mistake? And what is your biggest drawback?

Before this question, we have to solve this question that how does a person give birth to any kind of perception about another person?

No kind of perception can begin to form as long as you do not have any relationship with any other person. With any kind of relationship you have with any person, yours for that person and that person's for you, based on the events and situations happening in the past, present and future, different types of perceptions start being formed.

Here relationship means that you know another person in any way, having a different image of that person from other people printed in your mind, you have any kind of identifying information related to that person.

If I take the help of characters and names to describe this thing better, then any of your friends, your love, your parents, your near and far, in whatever range your relatives present, your neighbours, People related to your work who is known as your co-workers in your office and most important of this chapter your business relationships, which may be of any kind, good, bad, customers who ask for credit, the value on time Paying customers, everyone associated with that business.

Along with all this, you are emotionally, physically, socially, financially which will be called commercially, in all these forms your relationships with all these different types of people are connected. Relationships are connected, it means that any level of information, identity, thought, personality is stored with these people in your hearts, minds, for each other, in the form of perception, Whatever has happened between you and them and is about to happen, all those perceptions are formed based on these events and circumstances.

Now your mind will be tired for a while in understanding all these highest level things and you must have sipped a hot tea to overcome this fatigue, and only then you will get the idea that This writer is getting me caught in the web of meaningless words. Where there was talk of a shortage subject, suddenly I am spending my time in understanding the issue of perception. If you have drunk your tea completely, then here I will say that I am not turning you around, but the question of perception I have written in the answer is directly related to our question of lack and mistake. Let's understand this how.

So far we have understood the perception side, so considering that as the basis, let us look at an example. Let's say that you are watching your favourite show at your home, lying on your most comfortable sofa. At the same time, without taking permission from you and your enjoyment, I enter the atmosphere of your happiness and after that, I come to you and leave with a loud slap on your soft cheeks. A few days after the day this amazing incident happens to you, I will bring my special tea bag to your house. I give you information about its reasonable price and quality and request you to buy that tea.

Now I ask you the question that will you buy that special tea?

Maybe you are the biggest tea lover in this world, even then you will not buy that tea from me, but you will slap me tightly, maybe you will start beating me badly and it is also possible that Seeing me, your anger increases so much that you can call your neighbours and start the program of beating me, and maybe you can also include some police officers in this program.

You might not like this slap woven example, but this example explains the topic of my "perception" quite well. When I came to your house without knocking and slapped you, at that very moment a perception was born for me in your hearts and minds, and the day I brought my special tea to you to sell, That day you did not pay attention to that tea. That day you did not give importance to my business work, That day, instead of giving importance to your love for tea, you decided to put all these aside and on that day you decided to give full importance to the perception related to me only in your heart and mind.

Now many of you will stand in support of this perception and say that it is right, how can someone enter my house and slap me without any reason, and How can I buy tea from such a bad person? Here it is not a matter of good or evil. Here it is not a matter of morality and immorality. If it were about this, I would have stood with you too. But here is the point of your perception, due to which the real attention that my business was supposed to get was not received. Yes, I was solely responsible for the formation of this bad perception. But not every perception needs to be born in this way.

Many times most of the perceptions are born indirectly, even if you do not want to, because of the events and circumstances that happen through kind of relationship you have with a person, In the mind of that person, a perception of you has been made or is about to be made. The effect of which you will not feel in ordinary life, but you will start seeing its effect when you go to that person to get attention for any of your important work, that too thinking that I have a good relationship with this person. , then this person will give more importance to my work than the rest. But if any perception related to you sitting in the heart and mind of that person is negative, then obviously it will harm your important work as well.

To understand this better, I would like to present another example, which will try to explain to you in a special way that How indirectly perceptions are created.

Suppose there is a group of some friends. Their friendship goes back centuries, so much so that they do not need to maintain any permission, invitations and a good demeanour to visit each other's homes. These people whenever they want to go to any friend's house and enter into any personal space of his house, and on this negligence, the members of that house also do not feel bad. If some such people will have such friendship with each other, you can think for yourself that, what will be the amount of trust in each other in their group? That is hard to guess. Well, we have come to know how deep friendship these people have with each other. Now it's time to test that friendship.

There is such a person in the group of friends, who is always joking. This person has never given importance to any person, any important thing and any important activity in life. Always takes everything lightly and enjoys life like a game. For this reason, even the marks in the report cards received from all his schools did not give much importance to him. His friends are aware of his attitude from school days to youth. His friends only think about him that this person is always fun, joking, roaming around and thinks of taking pleasure from everything, This person can never be serious.

If you are fond of reading books, it does not mean that you must have never seen any movie, must have seen and must have seen a lot. Just like every film has a twist, in the same way, there was a twist in this story as well and along with it the sense of understanding of this person also emerged.

Many people are intelligent since childhood. They have to do some important activities which are necessary for their life, such as earn their education from a school with great seriousness, for which such people do not need to be reprimanded, shouted and punished by any well-wishers. Such people, while staying in their natural posture, do everything with ease.

But it is also important to recognize that not everyone is like this. No person is such a sensible person from his childhood. He does not take his life seriously from the very beginning. When the taunts of people, the sad face of the family, the stumbling block and the importance of loved ones start getting less in life, then that funny person gets hurt in his heart and from that moment that person decides that I will answer the questions of the whole world not by speaking but by the success of my work.

This person also realized that now in my life I have to do some work of my own. How long will I be sitting on my parents' trust? For how long will I keep listening to the poisonous taunts of family members and relatives? Now I have to take care of myself and my family.

Amid all these serious thoughts, he thought of starting his own business. He thought that people are not getting any washing powder to satisfy their hearts, minds and pockets these days. Some washing powders in the market prove to be good in washing clothes but their price is not according to the pockets of all people. I have such an idea that I will bring that type of washing powder in front of people which also fulfils the real purpose of washing clothes and also greatly reduces the expenses of people to buy any washing powder. With this good idea, that funny person started his business. The washing powder produced in his business initially got a positive response, with the hope that he reached the house of his wonderful friends with lots of packets of his better washing powder, And going there, he started telling the definition of his business to his friends, with the hope that whether someone else should give attention to my initial work or not, these people are my good friends. These people will support me to move forward. Will buy my special quality washing powder.

What do you think his best childhood friends will support him in this business or not?

If you answer this question based on goodness, morality, friendship, then you will say yes to it. But keeping these aspects in mind, if every person started doing all his actions, then perhaps today we would never have met words like deficiency, mistake, evil and important "negative perception" associated with today's chapter.

You must quite agree that in the world only good feelings do not rule. Bad feelings such as "negative perception" also exist among people, which are directly and indirectly born by any person or people or group. You also have to understand that negative perception of any person, thing or service, being born in your mind is not always bad and such a belief does not always support good results in your future.

Like the slap example, I presented to you, In that, I was directly responsible for the perception of anger that was born in your mind and I think it's bad fruit, my tea not getting attention from you, was very important that day. If you did not show me the effect of that incident on that day, then perhaps my courage would have increased, and it may also be that on the next pleasant day, I would do the same thing with you again. But it is not only necessary to give your angry reaction to that bad action, but with that reaction, you also have to know why I did that kind of thing to you? After listening to that reason, you can decide whether you should buy my tea or not. But I also know that as I have given the example, even if there is a person like an enlightened soul in the same situation, then he too will definitely get angry at such a bad act and will not even pay attention to my tea. It may be that after a few days the anger of that enlightened soul person may cool down and knowing my valid reason, maybe buy my tea after I request him a lot.

This was a direct form of the birth of a negative perception which sometimes becomes beneficial support for the future decisions you make. From bad people like this tea seller or any bad long-term experience acquired by you through the consumption of such product and service, which has given rise to a negative perception of you about the product and service, Which will later serve to save you from re-consumption of that bad experience product and service.

But what about those perceptions which arise indirectly in the mind of any person, for any other person, even if they do not want to, and which may not prove beneficial for you or that person in the future.

As the second example, I presented, in which I asked you a question that "What do you think his best childhood friends will support him in this business or not?" To which I am going to answer now. Match your answer. Perhaps after coming this far, your answer also matches my answer.

So the answer to this question is, his friends did not give even a pinch of attention to that funny friend (who is now very serious about his life). Instead, these people did not have to buy that washing powder, so they handed over a list of excuses from around the world to that funny person, and after that friend left, they started making fun of him together. Started saying what business he would do, who till now has not been able to do any work properly in his life. He was always behind us in every field. Always had fun. Now we will take his washing powder. We do not think that this work is really necessary for him, maybe soon this business will be closed.

So this was the kind of thinking that the funny turned serious guy's friends had towards him. Those who had taken such an image of that business person in their hearts and minds, which was completely harmful to the person who wants to move ahead in his life, but this belief was not going to benefit those people. Perhaps later on these people will have to bear the loss in the form of losing their funny friend.

Make a Black list of your customers.

So with this, I am giving such a golden tip to all of you who are associated with any business activity or are going to join in future, Which will help you find the right customers for your business who deserve your attention and time, And at the same time, your business-related disappointments will drastically reduce.

> *"This hidden rule of all types of business in the world is that your business will never benefit from your unbreakable relatives, your best friends, and your dearest neighbours."*

After reading this tip, you do not have to start abusing me that what kind of author is this who is making us away from our dear and piece of the liver like friends, relatives and neighbours. You are wrongly thinking that I am distancing you from them, but this is a wonderful truth received by all the businesses in the world, which emphasizes that every business, no matter how small or how big, always benefits from unknown people. Close people are always seen at food and drink parties.

Do not get angry after reading this or start telling your own stories that this has not happened to us. In the use of every thought, every deed, every object and service, its exceptions are present with him from the beginning, Which is waiting to get your attention. If we do not look at the exceptions, walk with good thinking and especially by holding the hand of the truth and moving towards the destination,

Then these three types of customers make every business run on a real scale.

1. People who have come to you because of the attractive marketing of your business product or service.

Marketing is a tool by which you find the right kind of customers for your business. It doesn't matter whether he is your friend or not, relative or not, neighbour or not, you only give information about the quality of those goods and services through the marketing of your business and Explaining the reason why people became your buyers, and people who have any negative perception related to you in their mind, then through your effective marketing, the effect of that perception will also be less on these people, when these people will come to buy your business product and service.

2. People who have come to hear the praise of the product or service made or sold by your business.

Now when you will work sincerely to do effective marketing of your business, then more or less the number of people will become your customers and the customer who will become it means that they will consume the products and services related to your business. The experience of which can be good or bad for these new customers, depending on the quality of your product and service. If the quality of your product and service is liked by your new customers, if they are completely satisfied with you then the effect of this will be that you will get more new customers for your business in future. Quickly increase the size of the safe, because people who have liked your product and service very much will appreciate it from their friends, relatives and neighbours. No doubt about it. These have become your customers who have come after hearing the praise of your business.

3. People who see their needs and your product or service together.

Such customers are like rain without season. which no one can expect. Nor have such customers seen any marketing related to your business. The way of their arrival is such that a sales store of products and services related to your business is established at someplace and a person passes through that place. When he sees your products and services and asks his need whether I should take it, or a person may ask his desire that should I consume them? and if a very intelligent person passes by then he will ask himself whether I can take those products and services along with my desire.

If all these people answer yes to all the questions asked by themselves, then understand that they are going to be the new and maybe last time customers of your business. Because they may not pass back from that place or it may be that they are satisfied with your products and services but they live far away from your place of business.

- **Just the essence of the thoughts so far is to pay attention to your own and other people's perceptions, if possible try to change them. Spend your time and attention on the right types of customers for your business, who will truly benefit you. Other exceptions are present everywhere. It depends on you to walk with good thinking and truth.**

Part Two: Let's do some religious talk.

If you do not want to fight in the name of your beloved religion, do not instigate anyone else, then let's learn some useful things from your religion.

TWO

HOW TO ORGANIZE HINDUS?

I am 100% sure that many people's faces must have turned red with anger after reading this title. Especially those people who do not believe in any particular religion. Who treats all religions and castes equally. Those people who want to establish humanity as a religion. So for those people who have such brilliant ideas. I want to say my point clear to them that I am also trying to adopt these qualities.

- I do not believe in any kind of discrimination.
- I respect every religion and every ethnic person.
- And as far as I am concerned about writing on this title today, the experience I got a few days ago has compelled me to write such an article.

So let me introduce you to the compulsion because of which you are angry right now, but trust me, your anger will completely end after reading this article.

My father is the main member of Rashtriya Swayamsevak Sangh. Instead of telling you the complete details of my father here, I would like to introduce you to the incident which is mainly related to this article. And as far as knowing about the SANGH, you must know that the SANGH is such an organization that is known to organize the Hindu citizens of India, propagate Hinduism and stop the influence of non-Hindus.

After giving the initial information, now I connect you with the main words of this article. It was afternoon, I was busy with some work at my shop, which works I do not want to bore you by telling you in this article.

Then the Pracharak of the Sangh of Banswara region came and sat on my shop chair. I called my father, talked sweetly and at the same time took the pleasure of sweet tea. It was during this time that he and I were introduced and after spending some time at my shop, he realized his responsibility which was given to him by the Sangh with great expectations, that is to promote the Sangh. He tried to know from me about my closest friends and among those friends, I introduced him to one of my best friends but there most of the talks or it would be correct to say that I and my friend debated, that too on that subject on which the Pracharak of the Sangh himself wanted to speak. That subject was religion.

After this incident, the Sangh Pracharak was very pleased with me and my friend because we are young and have good public interest, so after a few days, the Sangh Pracharak called me and offered himself a lunch invitation at my home. Then do all the good things and enjoy good food.

After this, my purpose of writing this article begins because after this lunch when I and the Sangh Pracharak were leaving my house, he again remembered their responsibility which was given to him by the Sangh. Realizing the responsibilities means fulfilling the tasks related to the purpose of the Sangh and you must have come to know in the initial part of this article what is the purpose of Rashtriya Swayamsevak Sangh. For the fulfilment of those objectives, a plan came to his mind as soon as the Pracharak of the Sangh left my house and after going some distance from my house he told me his plan of mind.

The Pracharak of the Sangh took me along, introduced me to the youth of my age and told the youth of my age and me about the plan due to which we were travelling to contact people. The purpose of that plan was that the next day all the youth of my area should be gathered and Sangh and the objectives of the Sangh should be told to all those youths so that these young people can also join the Sangh as a worker. Make their contribution, The more people who join the Sangh, The more people who will consider the words of the Sangh as an order, the sooner the objectives of the Sangh will be fulfilled. Keeping this in mind, I and the youth of my area gathered at a designated place at the behest of the Sangh Pracharak. The meeting started with the introduction of every person present in that meeting and in the end, the Sangh Pracharak started using the words which he was taught in the Sangh. That is to say, to convey the real objectives of the Rashtriya Swayamsevak Sangh to the young people who came to that meeting.

Now, without completing the garland of these stories, let me take you directly to the question that is why you are reading this article today. The RSS Pracharak, while giving his speech, asked the question to all the people present there that how should we organize Hindus? Every person tried to answer that question with his understanding and experience in life, but no one could satisfy the Pracharak of that Sangh with his answer. Even I could not answer that question but that question is still lingering in my mind, the result of which is this article. Yes, then I could not answer this question but I want to answer it through this article.

How to organize Hindus?

Before answering this question, we should know about Hindus.

A Hindu person is not just a Hindu as is the case with other religions. As a person of the Muslim religion is only Muslim, he is not divided into castes like people of the Hindu religion. Being divided into castes means that the people of the Hindu religion are divided into different castes. Like some Rajput caste, some Brahmin caste, some Bhil caste, some Jain and in that too there are two types of Jains, first Digambar and second Shwetambar. Due to being of different castes, they have different societies, they have temples of their totem deities, and those totem deities can be worshipped only by the people belonging to that particular society, such an indirect form has been made. Every person does it on his level.

If a society is formed separately, then it is obvious that some of its heads must have been appointed by the people of the society, whose job is to do the work related to the interest of the society and to make rules and orders from time to time for the benefit of the society.

The reason for being a separate society is the different thinking of that society, different customs, different beliefs and different ways of worshipping God, which is largely different from other castes of Hindu religion.

After knowing the difference of so many Hindu religions, now we come to our question that how to organize Hindus?

Before answering this question in your mind, a question should be that why should Hindus be organized?

If you ask this kind of question, then it shows your good understanding because there is a purpose for doing any work, no matter what it is. Without knowing the purpose of any work, without knowing the result of any work, what will be good for me by doing this work?

- If I am not getting any good by doing this work, then is someone else getting good?
- Do I have that much capacity and desire that I can do good to someone else?
- If I do not have that much capacity and desire to do this work, then how can I do this work?
- If I have the ability and desire to do this work as much as I need, then my next question should be, is there any harm to anyone, which I feel is good work by doing this work?

If you also make effigies of such questions inside your mind before starting any work, then you will be seen as an aware citizen of this country who does not do any work without thinking.

Then the same question, why is it necessary to organize Hindus?

- Because the more people of the Hindu religion stay organized, the more they will stick to their religion. They will not come under the influence of any other religion.
- It will be easy to reach the ideas of the Hindu religion to all the people.
- People associated with the Hindu religion will live their life according to the rules prescribed in the Hindu religion.
- The more united the people of the Hindu religion, the more they live in unity, the more they will be able to know each other's situations of happiness and sorrow, and the more the people of Hindu religion will have information about each other, the more people of Hindu religion will know about each other. Will be enthusiastically involved in

happiness and will be able to help each other in sorrow according to their ability and desire.

Overall, if we take out the essence of these things written above, then we want to do good to other human beings on the side of humanity, the only difference is that the help has been given the name of a particular religion or it can also be said that a particular religion is only thinking about the welfare of the people of its religion.

"But we have to remember only the word "good" and forget all other names and definitions.
"

So after reading this article till now, we have come to know that organizing Hindus, means doing good to the people associated with the Hindu religion.

Here again, a question arises that we want to do good to the people associated with the Hindu religion, but Hindus are divided into castes.

It is not like any other religion, that whatever my religion is, it is my caste. Then the same thing happened again and again that we have to organize Hindus for this, Hindus will have to forget their castes and consider only Hindu religion as their caste.

- People have to leave their society and focus only on building Hindu society.
- People will have to gather their chief and appoint one chief who can lead this entire Hindu society in a true sense and maintain unity among Hindus.
- Except for the worship of different faiths, beliefs, customs and different totem deities, one has to be involved in the devotion of Mother India only.

How easy it was for me to write these things on a blank paper with my lovely pen without any trouble amidst the pleasant breeze, sitting on a chair covered with a velvet cushion. But implementing these things in the right way on the ground is like playing the bugle of the war of Mahabharata.

Even you knew this part of this article, you knew all this information related to the Hindu religion in one way or the other. I have not mentioned anything new in this. The purpose of every article written by me is not limited to giving such information on a subject matter that you can gather in a moment by the fast internet of your smartphone, but the purpose of every one of my articles is to tell the problems of any subject matter. After that, there is an attempt to give a better solution to it. In this article also I am trying to take you towards that effort of mine.

If you don't mind and your faith in this religion is not hurt in any way, then I request that you have to forget some important things till the last word of this article, then only you will be able to recognize the efforts of this article. You should forget about Hindu religion, society, its special name, unity and most importantly, "How should we organize Hindus?" This question will have to be forgotten until the completion of this article.

If we forget these things for a while and consider the existence of societies associated with the Hindu religion for now, then because people associated with the Hindu religion are more proud of their society than being a Hindu.

- Gives more recognition to his society.
- They try to follow the thinking and customs of their society.
- They believe more in establishing and maintaining the unity of their society.
- They intend to get sympathy from the people of their society.

Whereas all these things should not be expected from any particular society, but considering Hindu religion as one and last society, one should expect from it only. But my writing in this way will not make any difference because even before me, many knowledgeable and very special people standing in the interest of Hindus have tried to bring people associated with the Hindu religion in unity through different mediums. Therefore, I do not want to contribute anything to this effort, but I want to contribute to those works, which will indirectly work to organize Hindus.

If a person decides that from today I will do good to the people associated with the Hindu religion,

In all their troubles, according to my ability and desire, I will help them and I will reach the idea of my great Hindu religion to the people. So such a person should not start this kind of welfare work with any Hindu person.

Yes, I am promoting casteism here but you cannot justify me wrong without completing this article. If a person thinks that he wants to do good work according to his ability and desire, then he should start it with the people of his society.

Because if I helped someone who is of Hindu religion but not of my particular community then what do you think will be the next part of the story?

I helped such a person with my welfare thinking, who is not from my society, so the people of my society will not praise me for this work. My felicitation ceremony will be held in front of the people of the society whom I have helped. Help can be of any kind whether it is financial, whether it is saved from going in a bad situation, anything that I needed to do that help for that person and for that person's society. So which society do you think I will make happy at the end of this story?

It is obvious that that person and if the act of helping will be useful for that person's society, then that society will be happy and if a situation came where my intention to help was good, but on the contrary, I got into trouble, while helping that person.

I will again give you a chance to guess what mode will this story take now?

Now in this, there will be less chance of sympathy and help in the story, on the contrary, the roles of different types of villains will be seen. The society you claim to belong to will not support you in any way in this problem, on the contrary, you will be blamed, they will taunt you,

- Why did you help any other person or people of the society?
- If you had the ghost of becoming a social worker, you would have contributed to your society.
- Now you have made a mistake, suffer it.

These are those sentences that you will not find in any such book which teaches you the way of living life in the right way. In such books, the good things are more and less are mentioned about the true events on the ground so that there is no disappointment in any reader.

Every writer has his different thinking, he tells it through the experience he got in his life. In the same way, I also have a thought that we should not run away from our shortcomings and neither should we accept them and go completely into the darkness of despair. Rather recognize your shortcomings and face them, Those shortcomings should be accepted and better measures should be thought of to overcome those shortcomings.

If you also accept the evil of "casteism" associated with your Hindu religion and try to find better and better ways for it, then it simply means that you should do the work of human welfare at the level of your society, so that there will be no hindrance in the work of human welfare. The people of your society will be happy with you and encourage you for your work and if you ever get into any trouble, then your whole society will try to get you out of that difficulty.

Here you must be feeling that this article is completely a source of promoting casteism but how can you make this decision without knowing my purpose completely. For some time you should forget that I am only proposing you to help the people of your society. Instead, you should think that I have helped such a person who is associated with the Hindu religion as well as being of my society. So this proves that I have helped a person belonging to the Hindu religion.

Yes, I may not feel like I am helping a Hindu religion person while helping. Maybe when I was doing welfare work, I was looking at the name of my society. But just think, I have helped a Hindu person not directly, but indirectly. If we calculate it keeping in mind the subject of mathematics, then you have reduced one number from the population associated with Hinduism. It has become the same thing whether to hold the ear from here or from there, if we catch it, then we have our ear. With this thinking, it will be that those who want to contribute for the benefit of the entire Hindu society, their contribution will also be completed. They will get a goal that I have to help a certain number of people belonging to my particular society in my life. The fewer people the goal is to help, the sooner that goal will be accomplished, and if some person from each society has such an intention that "I have to help the people of my society in some way or the other according to my ability and desire. I want to convey the ideas of the Hindu religion." So the dream which we were seeing for the people of the entire Hindu religion, that dream is being fulfilled not directly but indirectly. So we should be happy and satisfied knowing this.

Now for those people who think of a secular country,

In which I am also involved, you can also help the people of your religion according to your convenience and according to your ability and desire, in whatever form that help. This thinking is not to promote casteism, this thinking is to set a goal according to our convenience, taking the subject of mathematics as the basis. So that we can help only the selected people at a fixed time.

> *"The smaller the goals, the quicker they will be accomplished."*

And only by fulfilling small goals, the big goal set by us will be fulfilled, which is to do good to the citizens of the whole of India. Therefore this work cannot be completed by any one person. For this, everyone will have to take responsibility at their level and select the citizens.

It is my request to you that you should not think of this article based on any particular religion, but keeping in mind the subject of mathematics, think in the interest of all the nation, because if you will help people of any caste or any religion in this country, then, in the end, It will be counted in the population of this country only.

THREE

THE ESSENCE OF ALL THE RELIGIONS OF THE WORLD.

Let us discuss some important points before starting this article because we have got an unshakeable, vague idea about our religion that no ordinary person can talk about religion. A normal person has the right to follow only religion without any question. Only some special persons have the right to think and talk about their religion like Guru, Scholar, Priest, Pastor and such a group that talks about protecting religion, only those people can talk about religion and express views about their religion.

If a common person gives his opinion on religion, even if his opinion does not harm the religion, even then that person is considered anti-religious in our society. These unusual, human-made rules are related to religion and also you should not be hurt by my words in any way, so I have written the real purpose of this article through some points below. So that you do not get furious just by reading the title of this article and do not start looking for the best utensils in your house to beat me.

1. Please don't get offended by this title.
2. I have no intention that you are going to know any kind of bad thing about your religion from this article or I have used any kind of bad words for your beloved religion through this article. Wipe your sweat off your face because there is nothing like that in this article.
3. In this article, I have not compared any particular religion with any other religion, such as which religion is great and which is not. I have no such

intention so please don't make any plans to kill me.

4. This is just my opinion. It is completely up to you whether you want to believe it or not.

5. One more thing I want to clarify is that I will use the word "religion" in this article but I am not going to discuss any particular religion in this article,

So I have a humble request that you please read all the words written in this article very carefully and after that, if you think that I am wrong, you may get a chance to tear my clothes.

The way I have tried to prove my innocence from the points written above, you must be looking at me as a cowardly writer, what kind of writer is this who can not write his words without fear. So for the sake of your knowledge, I keep my point of view on every subject freely, but religion is such a subject in which it is necessary to be afraid. Because religion is something else, through the path of religion, some people have interpreted religion for their benefit in such a way that every question asked by a curious innocent person is declared anti-religion.

In my observation, I have come to know that most people treat their religion as their son.

- Why am I saying this?
- Do I intend to challenge in this way the path made by the Supreme Lord?
- Is the purpose of my writing like this to offend you?

The answer to all these questions is complete no. I have no intention of disappointing you for your religious point of view. My point is that we treat our religion as if it is our son because when a person becomes the father of a son, who takes care of his son, brings him up with love, Gives him the knowledge of good and bad things in life. Studying which subjects in his son's student life will prove to be successful for his future, he repeatedly suggests taking that subject. A father also considers the career aspect of his son, while his son has the right to think on this subject, yet the father fulfils his role with love or even forcefully and how can we forget the married life where a father wants to bring his daughter-in-law to his home who is cultured, respectful of elders and gives a happy life for his son.

In this father-son relationship you have noticed one thing that a father takes care of his son, teaches, imposes his views on him, tells him what he should and should not do in life. In everything in life a father teaches his son from a young age to old age, he does not learn anything from his son. A father tries to teach his son whatever he has learned from his life experience, but what about his son's life experience? Yes, a son's experience cannot be more than that of his father, but do not give importance to that experience. To what extent is this right for you?

The father gives his knowledge to his son and does not intend to learn from his son because he felt that he is a father and a father need not take any advice from his son for life. This is the bitter truth of our life. All the people of the world follow this thing as a legal rule, such that if someone tries to break it, then he will have to face jail.

A father only thinks that he has a lot of experience so he needs to tell his life experience to his son but very few people listen to his son, they don't think that our son can think any right thing for his life That's why most fathers feel the need to impose their views on their sons. Most of the fathers think that sons have useless experience, so they do not attach any value to the life experience of sons.

> *"You don't think that every life experience is different and that everyone has some useful information from their experience. You only think about your idea, your experience is perfect."*

With this type of thinking process, you automatically prevent yourself from acquiring various useful knowledge.

Now your direct question will be that what is the relation of father-son relationship with religion?

If this question is arising in your mind then I am glad that you are going through this article very carefully. I have not discussed the father-son relationship in this article so that I can show you the truth of this relationship. This is not a topic today, but I want to describe here how we think about religion by taking this relationship as an example.

Just as you have seen the nuances of the father-son relationship above, in the same way we follow our religion with the same thinking. Now you must ask how?

Just as you have read above, a father only works to give to his son, whether it is love, knowledge, euphoria, thoughts, anger, sustenance, everything that a father can give to his son. Yes, he gives his son from time to time but does not learn anything from his son. Now many people will get annoyed by the fact that we have listened to our son, so I am not talking about all the fathers of the world here for your knowledge. I want to say that most fathers do this.

Similarly, you treat your religion as a father treats his son. You tell your religion "How great you are, your reach is very high, you are very special, your status is the highest, I will protect you, I will impose your upper cover on people, but not your thoughts. You are a great religion, you will be worshipped by everyone, but if someone refuses to worship you, Then I will punish him like your keeper."

You have seen that somehow you play your role like a father and look after your religion like a son. A father feels that his son cannot make the right decisions in his life, so a father decides on every aspect of his life with his own understanding instead of his son. Just as most of the fathers work only to teach their sons, in the same way, you also work to teach your religion while you should learn from your religion. Only you should focus on the study of religion by not accepting it on the upper side.

The question never came to your mind that the religion I glorify. I take pride in being it and when I feel that my religion is in danger, I go out to fight for it to any extent.

- What is so in that religion?
- Have I done some good work in my life with the words of that religion?
- Have I followed the things written in the books of my religion in my life?
- Or I have set out to protect religion only for show or at the behest of someone else.

This is the same as you are in the tenth class in your student life and you have not studied any subject throughout the year and at the end of the year, you are going to take the exam. What do you expect from yourself that you will pass that exam. No, not at all. In the same way, you should see religion as a book of knowledge, after studying the things of which you can become successful in the examination of your life. But in today's era, ignorant people use it as an intoxicant. As soon as there is any mention of their religion, they become furious without thinking and in that fierceness, they do their own harm.

Now coming to the real purpose of this article is to give you the essence of the world's religions.

- What do I mean by summarizing the religions of the whole world?
- Have I studied all religions?
- And now I am going to prepare an outline of all religions in front of you through my acquired knowledge.

No, I haven't done any study. You may be angry that then how can I write the essence of the religions of the whole world. You will find the answer to this question at the end of this article. So the essence of all religions stands on these three things. Now you must be thinking that is there any God in me who has created religions for the welfare of human beings? Yes, you are right but I am a worried human being and thinking thoughts related to every human life, Who has given suggestions from his experience to do these three things in human life at the necessary level.

Yes, this is my suggestion which is not part of any constitution, if you do not follow it, you will have to face legal troubles.

First of all,

You must think about it in your life on the side of a human that, by my work, by my thinking, any human, animal, creature on a mental level, on an emotional level, financially, on a physical side and is there any harm happening on the social side? If you contemplate this work and have been doing this work till now in your life or are thinking of doing it then good luck you are walking on the path of your religion.

> *"No religion will ever stop you from doing good deeds, will always ask you to think about the other."*

Second Job,

- Can I do well for myself and my family in this beautiful life by my work, by my thinking?
- Can I help myself and my family?
- Can I move ahead in life through my work?

This is the work which is related to your duty, which every religion tries to say by some means that you should continue to do your duty, which you have got the responsibility and that duty should be done in such a way that you can move forward in your life, do good to yurselves and your families.

Third Job,

- Can I contribute in any way to the welfare of this human society through my work, through my thinking?
- Can I help someone with my work?
- Whether that help is from any medium, such as financially, emotionally, mentally, socially, in whichever medium in which I can contribute by my ability and my full will.
- Can I show someone the right path in life through my thinking?

If the answer to all these questions is yes, then you are walking on the path of religion.

> *"I do not think that any religion in the world will ever deny these three works because all religions talk about doing good to you and others through different means. The way of saying may be different, but all religions expect you to do good deeds."*

Part Three: Pick this Self Help book.

Try to understand your life from the point of view of my life, otherwise, this is all advice, others will also give it, you should ask your intellect as to which one to use.

FOUR

HOW CAN YOU OVERCOME YOUR LONELINESS WITHOUT UNDERSTANDING LONELINESS?

As soon as you read this question, your question may be that why should I even think about such a question? When I have to move away from this state of "loneliness", and from whom I have to go away, with whom I do not want to be with, then why should I waste my time in understanding that loneliness?

Having such thinking used to benefit you only when you were in your school days or are now. Because then you can do it during the school exam and especially when you did not study properly in the exam related to any subject to be held the next day. When you had fully guessed that I might be going to be killed soon by my father's hand because I am going to fail this time. Then a day before that exam, all the chapters related to that subject. Instead of trying to cover those chapters, which you can easily understand at that time and you can get such marks in that subject so that at the time of result you do not see fail written in capital letters in your report card.

This filtered thinking was probably very useful for you then, I agree, but this filtered thinking does not work in every aspect of life, Because the examination of life is not like the examination of any school, you want to study according to your mind and see the marks on your report card.

In life, you have to go through every part, every aspect, every situation and every dimension. Life has to be understood. have to deal with. Perhaps you do not see your disliked situation just by closing your eyes, but that wretched situation is watching you. She is standing in front of you right now, and if you do not prepare properly to fight her at the right time, she will defeat you and inflict a deep wound, the bad memory of which will defeat you in every part of your life.

And the thing is, you have to go away from someone, but what if some emotion or any person is stubborn. Even after you refuse him again and again, even after you request him, even after you repeatedly taunt him and say bad things, even if that person does not go away from you. He comes to trouble you every day. So to get away from such a person, you will think of some way, you will use some such strategy by which you can get rid of him, and to make that strategy, you have to understand him, have to know him completely. Which one should I do in such an act that he goes away from me quickly or what is the weakness of that person through which I can remove him from myself?

Similarly, this loneliness is also very stubborn. It always sticks with you. It keeps looking for opportunities in your life to show its effect on you or it will be right to say that you give it a chance to come into your life in every little trouble.

Loneliness = Stubborn Guest

A guest is someone who lives far away from you. You haven't seen him for a long time. You want him to come to your house. On this basis, whenever such an occasion comes to your house which is responsible for gathering a crowd of guests, then in that environment you invite your favourite and that distant guest to come to your house. You make a lot of requests to him, and sometimes you make emotional attacks on him so that he comes to your house by any means, only then does that guest step into your house.

But there is also a guest who happens to be a cumbersome neighbour of yours, whose arrival you are bored with, he has come to your house so many times. Wherever he has to go, his journey starts from your home. He just has to enter your house on some pretext or the other. Even if you don't treat him well, he tries to treat you well again and again. If there is such a guest as your neighbour and one day without giving much importance to that person like the rest of the guests, even if you have invited him to come to your house in a careless manner, even then, He would like to enjoy your hospitality at your home, leaving aside all his important work.

In the same way, your loneliness is also like that neighbour guest, who because of any kind of disappointment in your life, secures a ticket for his arrival in the house of your mind. So to get rid of such a strongly disliked guest, you have to understand him completely. His subtle weakness has to be recognized and attacked, only then will this stubborn 'loneliness' guest run away from your life.

Unravel the conspiracies

This is a big conspiracy or some big illusion which is spread in a huge amount by the people around you. Those people can be anyone, your parents, your relatives, your neighbours and your friends who claim to remove that loneliness or your dearest teachers of today i.e. Google and YouTube. On which the existing content is related to the truth, it depends on what kind of greed is hidden behind the teachings of the creator of that content.

Greed is not always bad either. Greed can also be of two types, bad and good.

Good Greed :

As someone is fond of taking applause by helping people, then you cannot call this type of greed bad. Because the motive behind this greed can be only to get applause or to hear a lot of praise. It does not matter, as long as some people are benefited by this greed in any way and they praise that person or ask good prayers for him, And that person also wants that people should call my name, again and again, thank me and always keep in me the feeling of being a special person. If there is a desire of such a person and through that greed, any kind of good is being done to the people of any society in the true sense, then such greed is very good. Because there is very little chance of causing any harm to anyone.

Bad Greed :

Bad greed is that which hunts some person or some people. Like why a hunter hunts any innocent animal in a forest? Had that hunted animal taken any loan from that hunter who could not get it back in time, then that hunter got angry and killed that animal and took his loan amount. If not, then what is the purpose of that hunter? The answer is that, any personal greed of that hunter, which is likely to be fulfilled by hunting that animal. What is the benefit of that animal? Will he get heaven instead of losing his life? Even if this happens, before hunting that animal, someone asked him, if I can kill you? Can I fill my stomach by killing you? Or can I earn my living by selling your meat? If that animal says yes on such questions, then it is fine, but without asking him to determine his future, that too such a future in which the advantage will be only of that hunter and the loss will be completely that of that innocent animal. You should not feel any shame in calling such greed bad greed.

So on the assumption of this greed, you have to recognize that whoever is the person or the forum of the Internet, who is giving the knowledge to escape from loneliness, then is there any greed behind it? If it is hidden, what kind of greed is it? good or bad? If it is good, as you have understood from the concept of upper greed, then there is nothing to worry about in it, but if there is bad greed, then you have to listen to it and ignore it.

If everyone's greed is a bad species, then which person will give me the knowledge of loneliness?

Me, whose greed along with personal selfishness also aims to help people. By personal greed, it means that the price you have paid to buy this book and the satisfaction I have got to express myself through this book is many times better for me than any other greed.

The meaning of help here is to help you in the right sense and while taking that help, you have to keep the idea of Buddha with you, because maybe from my thoughts you can give birth to such an idea with the use of your intellect. It may prove to be more beneficial for you. *(The thought of Buddha that you read on the opening page of this book)*

What is loneliness?

A person who is currently passing his time in this state of loneliness or who has gone through this situation. He sees that loneliness by connecting the subject of mathematics. He tries to find the reason for his hurt feelings by numbers.

As a person, he has felt loneliness in his life in recent times. He has come to know that the state of loneliness has started in my life, so I will have to be sad now. I have to try to get solace from the people around me by showing me my sad face. I have to try to sleep throughout the day so that I can not feel the loneliness that has come and when I wake up from my sleep, for some time, I can feel a sense of peace. That thing is different that after a few moments of that, I will go back to my state of loneliness. I will keep thinking about that loneliness and will think so much that during the night time it is time to sleep, I will wake up again and again and see from my window which person is happier than me and whether they deserve to be happy or not. I will declare my decision. Oh, this person deserves less than me to be happy, yet how is he so happy? Doesn't he feel lonely? Like I feel. God, what kind of illusion is this yours?

Maybe I know why I feel lonely?

The reason for this is that, in my life, people of my acquaintance do not live or live with me less, so I am feeling lonely in my life. That's why I am sad, and the happy person is happy because he has more people in his life. He has many friends, so he travels with those friends to many places of his choice. He has many relatives who take care of him every moment. He has good neighbours who share him in every conversation. How can such a person be unhappy who has more number of his people? Such a person can never feel lonely.

Now you have to know a truth that will greatly benefit your understanding of the subject of your loneliness, and that truth is that your loneliness never depends on the fact that you are with many people. Or you are feeling lonely by looking at many people from a window, that is, you are alone.

Your loneliness is born based on whether you can relate yourself with the environment around you, with different types of people, with their words and with all the things in this whole world. Whether you can create any kind of positive space in your mind for them or not. What kind of approach do you use when dealing with this world? Your loneliness will depend on that approach.

From these two bases, you see this world from your point of view and according to that, you decide for yourself that I will with this object, this service, this person, this situation, this result, this feeling and Do I have any connection with all the processes of my world that I face with time? If you have not been able to find this connection inside your mind, then you are definitely in the environment where you are now, feeling yourself alone.

To understand this better, first, let's talk about the bases from which your perspective of seeing this world is formed and based on which you can establish that relationship in your mind. Due to which you are less likely to feel lonely.

1. Your Choice

Your choice of any kind that corresponds to any person, any idea, anything and any environment or not, if your choice has made its place in all of them, then if you are even one in real numbers. Even if you are alone, you will not feel any loneliness.

Like, What's your favourite?

- What do you like to hear? And what are you listening to?
- How do you like to talk? And how are the people you meet talking to you?
- How do you expect people to treat you? And how do they treat you in return?
- What do you like to watch and what are you watching?
- Who do you like to be with and with whom are you spending your time at the moment?
- Which place do you like to go and where are you currently?

To understand this, even more, we take the help of a fictional story.

Like one day you went to such an event where you have no friend, no relative and no one person of your identity far and wide. All those who are there are unknown to you and you are unknown to them. Along with this, there is also a condition that in this story, your nature is not so friendly that you can quickly mingle with new and unknown people, become their friends and have a lot of laughs while staying together.

Now try to imagine this place where you are and you have to live among those people, Imagine your personality which is not soluble. If you further complicate the situation, then you do not like the performance of any artist going on before your eyes. It may be that the music used in that presentation is not of your taste. It may also be that the artist's presentation is not at the level you would like. Perhaps it may also happen that the way of behaving of the people sitting with you is different. Maybe their way of saying it is quite different from yours. There may be a lot of differences of opinion between you and those people. Maybe theirs and yours are very different in their way of looking at anything, and if so many differences have nothing to do with your choice, So you will soon feel lonely at that moment because the whole environment there is not according to you at all, so it is natural that a person tries to find his choice while doing every work. If that aspect of choice is found in that work, then along with the possibility of completion of that work, the possibility of getting pleasure from doing that work also increases.

"And where there is joy, there is no loneliness, even if you are really alone."

2. Your understanding

This is not the basis of good marks obtained from your school/college, but your understanding which welcomes all kinds of freedom, which is open-minded and if you take recourse to general definitions then an understanding which knows that Not everyone's preference is the same.

- One who knows that every person's way of expressing himself may be different because every person goes through a different type of experience and when he expresses himself, his experience is behind him, which can be good or bad.

- One who knows that not every person can understand every idea, most of the time the person agrees more on those ideas which he has experienced himself and that thought said by anyone only works to awaken a feeling in that person.
- In the same way, everyone's love for music can be different. Everyone can have a different type of entertainment and overall it is true that every human being has a different way of looking at the world from the rest of human beings.

One who understood this difference, who started welcoming this difference, that person can never feel lonely anywhere because he sees the likes of the people around him. He tries to be happy in their happiness. That person tries to learn something from everything different from his nature, and this constant curiosity of learning fills him with enthusiasm, because of which he never faces a situation like loneliness and even if he does. He quickly emerges from it.

It does not mean at all that you should forget your choice, you should decide the way of living your life according to someone else. As long as your path is moving towards Morality, legal scope and development, then you can follow the paths chosen by you, but when you realize that I am not able to see these aspects on my way, then this is your ultimate Have a duty and a right that you can learn from someone else And using your mental power on what you have learned, you can improve or change the path you have chosen.

Another reason for your loneliness. That is, you have no real purpose in your life.

The real purpose here does not mean to fulfil all the worldly desires that clash with age, in which the way to happiness is most of the time to achieve happiness by showing off all the material things you have achieved. Like an expensive car, luxurious house and beautiful life partner and many more your desires which are just made up for a show, which has nothing to do with real happiness. It's all meant to entertain you for a while but what about after that? The satisfaction that you try to get throughout your life through different experiments. But those experiments lead you to entertainment and short-term happiness but do not result in true satisfaction. That true satisfaction is hidden in the real purpose of your life.

That satisfaction is hidden in your question, whose answer you are looking for till date, that too through the most attractive teacher of today's time i.e. on Google, you type that how should I find my passion? With the hope that if Google knows everything, then it will also know what my passion is?

But you forget in your search of this question whether it is Google or YouTube, all these have been made by humans only, not by any miracle of God, where your trouble ends when you tell your problem.

> **"No matter how intelligent a person is, he cannot tell about your original personality unless you want to tell."**

You know what your passion is. What work do you enjoy doing the most? You know which work I like to do, even if I do that work for a long time, I do not feel any burden. I know that I keep thinking about that work every moment. I think of new ideas for that so that I can do better for passionate work of mine, that too not because I want to show that work to people and earn a lot of accolades or earn a lot of money. I know that the satisfaction I get while doing that work and the completion of that work, the happiness I get and the good feeling I always get from doing it, That feeling I will not get in return for any work in this world. I have a feeling for this deal.

Then why do I avoid giving that work the status of my "passionate work"?

When I asked myself "What is my passion?" So why can't I answer this question? It's because you have found your passion. Sometimes you are also collecting inner happiness from that passion, but external happiness you are not able to earn from that passion work in the present time. Like you are not able to earn enough money from your favourite work so that you can run your house, meet your basic needs and after those needs, you are not able to find even the fond things you look forward to.

You are not able to fulfil your financial purpose through your passion, due to which you are ignoring it even though your passion is with you or it may also be that you have not yet tried your passion work in the use of earning money. Perhaps till now, you are looking at your passion only as a means of entertainment or whenever you are bored, then you must be doing that favourite work. Otherwise, with all these ways to use your passion, you have not taken your passion seriously enough so that you can make your passion the only means of your livelihood.

Now coming to the question that has been going on in your mind for a long that what is the relation between my passionate work and my loneliness?

First of all, let's look at this maths equation so that you will not have to use much of your mental power to understand the ideas that come next.

- Your passionate work = Inner happiness + Inner satisfaction, Which is beyond the world.
- Loneliness is removed from your life by finding inner happiness + inner satisfaction.
- If you searched for your passion work or stopped ignoring it = Whenever you start feeling lonely then you will start doing your favourite work, so that you will not have to go through this newly arrived loneliness state.
- If you have not been able to find your passion work or are still ignoring it = You are given more chances for your loneliness to come into your life.

My story,

Even two years ago, I used to feel very lonely. I used to get bored very quickly with all the things around me. I always wanted something new, which would keep me excited. I used to feel lonely, so it does not mean that I was alone at the level of numbers, it was not like that at all, I was with my family and still am. The family that loves me very much. I had and still are very good friends, with whom I used to spend my time as per my wish. Had lots of fun. Everything was there, even then I felt quite lonely inside. The reason for this was not that I could not recognize my real purpose even after my many efforts, but the real reason for this is that which is yours. That is, I was also not able to fulfil my financial purpose with the work of my choice. That's why I used to ignore my passion work again and again. But when I felt a double dose of loneliness, that is, I was already feeling a lot of loneliness internally, along with it, the Government of India imposed a lockdown to prevent me from meeting the corona epidemic. I took double doses of this loneliness before taking the double dose of the vaccine. Then that loneliness pushed me towards my real purpose, which I had been ignoring till now due to my financial purpose not being fulfilled.

But the question comes at this stage of the story, what is my passion job after all? So that is writing. I was fond of writing since childhood, but earlier there was no definite purpose in my writing activities, whatever thought came to my mind, I would write it in the copies of homework given by my school, So sometimes I used to play my heart with words in a poetic style, and sometimes resorted to poems. But I do write in some way or the other.

After this came the time of 2016 which was going to give a direction to my passion for writing. In November of the same year, when I was reading a newspaper, my gaze stopped at a headline, in which it was written in big letters that the time has come when you are sitting at home through the Internet, You can do that work, from which you can earn a lot of money.

Now in the age of this greed, who would be such a person who cannot stop for a while after reading the word money, and cannot take further information. Yes, that thing is different, that most of the people read such remedies with thrill, but they do not use them in their life. I was also excited to read that information completely, and after reading the different ways to earn online in that newspaper article, my eyes fell on the advice which was directly related to my passion, that is, in that information. It was written that if you have a passion for writing, then you can earn good money sitting at home with this hobby and you can also quench your thirst for your writing hobby. For this, you just have to create your account on the blogging website by going to the Google search engine. After that, you will get the website of your favourite name, on which you have to write your thoughts on the topic that suits you best. If the more people come to your website, the more people will see or click on the ad placed by that blogging site on your website and you will be paid according to the rules of the blogging company.

So after reading this article I got very charged and immediately through the blogger website, after much thought I chose a name for my blogging website, that is Mirrorofobservation.com. After reading this, you must also be thinking that why did I choose such a name? Because it was written in that newspaper article that whatever subject you are more knowledgeable about, in which you feel that you can give good advice to people on that subject and if you write only on that one topic, whenever your readers faced any problem related to that topic, then they can try to solve their problem through the articles written on your website.

I thought a lot about it, on which subject am I good? So my mind said that leave it, you will not be able to do it. Because I was not so knowledgeable about any subject that I could write on it with authority. Then I thought I have to write and even if I was an expert in any one subject, I will not be able to do that work for a long time. Because I always want something new.

That's when I thought that whenever I felt like writing about any subject, any idea related to that topic came to my mind, then I will write my article on it. But I will not stop writing. That's why this subtitle of my website and this book is, "A mirror that sees everything, understands, thinks and writes its thoughts on it."

With so many understanding and encouraging things, I had started my official journey of writing, but it does not mean that from that day till today I have never stopped writing. Sometimes I would stop writing for days, weeks and even months. The reason for this was not that I was tired of writing, but I was so engrossed in my life in search of a definite career that I had never tried to see the hobby of writing as my career. I always used to watch it as a "time-pass", whenever I got free time and if I did not have any other means of entertainment, I used to sit down to write long-running thoughts in my mind.

But one rule of nature which I know from my own experience is that your real purpose is always with you. Even if you repeatedly say no to that purpose, it does not go out of your life. Your real purpose is the creator of such opportunities, which creates a movement from within you to do that purpose, and gradually that movement keeps on increasing within you, And it keeps on increasing until you start doing that purpose.

I had also realized this growing movement was in lockdown, then I used to pacify the movement going on inside me every day through my blogging website. I started writing on that website every day and started praising myself after reading what I had written earlier, started taking pride in myself (not vanity), which made me feel happy for myself. This encouraged me further and through which I recognized that my true happiness comes only from writing. I get real satisfaction from expressing my thoughts in writing. I know that I can do this writing work with great care and without getting distracted even for a while, I can do this work for hours. Whereas till date I used to get bored with all the work I have tried. I used to get frustrated with them when I did not get the result I wanted in return for my capable hard work. But when I write, I do not think about any result and the truth is that to date I have not got any such result that inspired me to write not one but two books. The result which we know as Financial Purpose. No such purpose of mine is being fulfilled by my writing skills. Even then I am very excited about this work. For this, I always think of new ideas, such as "I have to write on this topic today" and "I try to do better on the subject on which I have written." To do better, I wrote the first book of my life MY BEST WORDS and after that worked hard on this book which you are reading now.

Now you must be thinking that now I must have earned a lot of money from my first book, so I published the next book. No, it's not like that at all. I say again that none of my financial purposes has been fulfilled. Even then I am very excited about this work. I am very happy while doing this and always feel very satisfied after its completion. Because of this satisfaction, my mingling with people has reduced, even then I do not feel any loneliness. I am very happy inside because I am doing my real purpose. You do it too. If you haven't found your real purpose then seek it or stop ignoring it. Because after achieving that real purpose you will be away from the painful state of loneliness for the rest of your life.

FIVE

WHY DO YOU SAY THAT I AM IN LOVE WITH THIS PERSON?

When you meet love in your life, why do you say that I am in love with this person? This person is very nice to me. This person changed my life and many good things you say to everyone and especially through social media you post a cute picture of you and your life partner or maybe future life partner. you tell people about this good change in your life.

The thing is that you do not fall in love with a person at that time, rather you fall in love with your life at that time, which life was not so good before meeting that person as you are feeling good in your life now. The person you claim to be in love with is the person you tell the reason for the happy feelings in your life.

Instead, you should say that I have fallen in love with my life and you should post such posts on social media at that time that I have fallen in love with my life and of course, you should also post a picture with that social media post that is of your boyfriend or girlfriend. When you put such a post on social media, never forget to add your partner's picture with that post and don't misinterpret my words and give credit to your partner for this good change in your life. Don't forget. If you make such a mistake then your life and mine will become difficult. Perhaps your partner is sad because you are reading an article that encourages someone not to give credit for what has made a difference in your life.

If this happens, then I am just imagining the situation that your partner is sending me a derogatory letter and you are with your partner, then your partner will not send you a "non-readable letter" like me, but the letter which Your partner wrote for me, will do those things with you.

I don't want stuff like this. But I write in such a way that you should not tell people that you have fallen in love with your partner, rather you should say that I have fallen in love with my life. There is a strong reason behind this, that is, Because when you had no hope that someday you would meet a person who would change your life the way you feel today. When you were so lonely in life. When you were not able to enjoy your life as much as you are enjoying it today. Whatever you thought before this, everything was not so good. When any need of your body like physical, mental, emotional was not being met.

So you were passing through this kind of story and one day a person passes by you and like the fragrance of flowers fills your life with fragrance. That person also had the same feelings that were jumping inside you at that time. You both met each other and came to the conclusion that you both are each other's soulmates.

After that, you publish this important piece of information about your life like "I have fallen in love with this person" and together there is a beautiful picture of the two of you. So I have to say that if you look carefully at all these things then you are not happy because you have a lovely person. You are not so excited because you meet your soul mate. You are happy because your life changed at that time. You feel so good at that time. You start behaving the best at that time. You expect everything to be good for yourself at that time. It is not all because you have met a person of the opposite sex in your life. All this because you feel special at that time.

You are freed from the worries related to your body's needs that were troubling you earlier. Like physical, mental, emotional, social, you have made a perfect plan in your mind to fulfil all these needs, which you will fulfil slowly by your partner. And because of that at that time you feel great, you think well, you behave well, you expect everything to be good for you. You don't even think about a sad situation for a moment in that love time.

Every time you smile, sometimes your well-wishers show concern for your unrealistic regular smile. After this passion of yours, your life changes because you change your environment by giving initiation by a person and with your thinking you make that environment even better. Your way of thinking is more important than the person whom you consider to be the reason for the big change in your life, whereas, in reality, you should give credit to your thinking for this good change in your life, due to which your whole life becomes better.

"It is all because you have changed your thinking pattern, because of this you should say that I have fallen in love with this person instead of saying that I have fallen in love with my thinking or I have fallen in love with my life..."

SIX

EDUCATIONAL QUALIFICATION = EXPECTATION

Is there any information regarding the educational program that I want to inform you and I request you to join this program as soon as possible? No, I have no such intention. But the thing is that your education certificate is not just a piece of paper or a document which you always show to different interviewers from different companies to get a good job and not only for your proof that you are not an illiterate person. These are all basic information that you know about using your educational certificate. If you want to know more details about what situations your educational certificate can help you. If your curiosity says yes then read this.

Your education qualification decides your work. Perhaps after reading this line, you will say that I know this thing. What's new in this? Then I want to say wait. The story does not end here. You must be thinking that your education qualification determines your work, this sentence is correct. But you are looking at this sentence only from the point of view of getting a job in a reputed company, while many other works. As you can be a successful business owner after completing your graduation. Or you can work in a service sector Or maybe you are manufacturing products or a lot of different products in your factory. Maybe you are earning good money from your singing, Maybe you can be a famous painter.

You can choose any such work after the completion of your studies, which does not match at all with your studies. This can happen. There are many such examples which can change the myth that you should get a good job after getting an education certificate from your college and especially you should look for work in the same field for which you did higher education.

You know your talents, you know your abilities, you know what jobs you like and dislike. You always have an option to change your mind after your graduation or maybe after your post-graduation. Is there any such rule written in our constitution that you have to follow the work you have studied in college life? No, there is no such rule. So what's the problem with your people, the people around you? Your relatives, friends of your friends, and friends of your parents are always ready to do their duty of giving advice.

It does not matter whether their advice is useful to you or not or whether you like that advice or not. They don't think about it. They only perform their duty and force you to follow their given advice in your career aspect.

Let us understand the game of your people,

Who always played with you. Let's say that when you were a teenager, you were not so much interested in studies but you were interested in doing some work. That's why you chase this dream. It may also happen that your financial condition is not so good at that time so you could not do your further studies and now you have the only class tenth certificate. In this story, all those so-called people who claim that they are your well-wishers, don't come to you to give you the best career advice about what they like and what they think you need to be successful in your life, you should follow the path shown by us.

No, they don't come to you because their rule of giving career advice to others says that you should give your valuable career advice to those people who have a better educational certificate in their pocket, If not then you have no right to give your advice to such people. Because these are the people who judge your character aspect from the aspect of your education qualification. If you are good at studies then your relatives, friends of your parents and your well-wishing neighbours will consider you a good boy by nature, by your behaviour.

> *"You may have a good educational qualification but it does not prove that you are a good person."*

These two things are quite different from each other. One aspect of this is about your knowledge of various subjects in your school and college and the flip side of this is about the subject of moral science. This is not a compulsory subject in our education system, in which if you don't study it then your marks may get less in your result, no, there is no such condition. Studying the subject of moral science depends on the efforts of your teachers whether they take this subject seriously for you or not. It depends on your parents that how they raised you in childhood and what kind of education they gave you. It depends on your friendzone which you always try to follow to be a cool guy. You do not think in your childhood whether your friends are good or bad and what they teach you is good for you or not. You follow them blindly because at that time you are also a child and a child does not have that much understanding of right and wrong.

Your certificate of education not only determines your character, but also the kind of work your well-wishers expect from you, the kind of studies you have done. If you go from back, we came to that example where you have only 10th class certificate, after that you could not do further studies due to any circumstance. Therefore, your well-wishers will not expect better work from you and will not give you any advice to achieve success in life. Overall you can say that they will not bother you because these people have a level to advise you or harass you.

If you are only passing in class ten then you can do anything in your life. No one will stop you, not your parents, not your neighbours and not your best well-wishers. Because they have already put this thing in their minds, now nothing can happen to you because you have not studied as these people wanted from you. Yes, it may be that you are repeatedly taunted for being illiterate, even when you are probably doing better work in life than these people. But no one will even expect you to do anything good in life.

But if you have studied till class 12,

then the level of expectation of these people from you will increase. These people will insist on you to study further. Suppose you have studied science in class 12, then these people will ask you to study doctor or engineer. Whether you want to go ahead in that subject or not, it doesn't matter. In the same subject, you have studied, these people will expect you to move ahead only in that subject and not any other subject and suppose you have studied one subject completely by mistake. Suppose you have completed your studies as a lawyer, then these people will chant on you in such a way that you will not be able to think of anything other than this line.

Maybe you have studied lawyer only according to the acquisition of knowledge, It may also be possible that on the insistence of your family, you have done such a study, And it may also happen that you like this topic at the time, but now your mind is to go to some business field. There is no such rule that you have to earn money in your life through what you have studied and if you do not do this then you will be entitled to sin. That's why I wrote the title of this article in such a way that educational qualification = expectation.

"*The kind of study you do in your life, that kind of hope gets attached to you."*

The less education you have, the fewer people will expect from you and it can also be said that the fewer people will trouble you. You will be able to do whatever you want in your life. No one will stop you by taunting you.

But this whole chapter does not mean that you should not get any kind of education in your life. If you are thinking this after reading this chapter, then you are thinking wrong because not only do we make such a paper by education, so that we can get a job in a good company, but through education, we can put our point in front of people in a good way. If you do not know the right words or sentences or such things, due to which you cannot tell your point well to anyone, even when your thinking is right at that time, even then that person whom you want to tell your point, he will be away from you. With education, we can write well so that the one you want to get your point across can understand your real feeling. Yes, it is definitely that you should study about the field in which you want to work later so that you can do well in that field. Education is Important.

The purpose of this chapter is to make those people realize their sins, who play the role of a well-wisher around you but they knowingly or unknowingly do many inauspicious things with you. Especially from your childhood till your youth, their taunts are involved in most of the decisions. The result of which is that you fail in many decisions taken by you, because you do not take all those decisions with your understanding and choice, Rather, you are forced to take all those unsuccessful decisions under the pressure of sinful advice of those well-wishers.

Now after reading this, do not make again any wrong opinion in your mind that you should not follow any advice of any of your well-wishers. No, I do not mean anything like that, but at the very beginning of this book, I have already told you the idea of Buddha. According to which you have to take full of advice and knowledge from everyone, but when the time comes to take decisions in your life, then you have to use your understanding.

SEVEN

WHAT ARE THE FIRST THINGS TO THINK ABOUT BEFORE DOING ANY WORK?

How does a job start? It means what is the first step you should take when you are going to start any work. Any work can mean anything, any thought that is running through your mind right now. You can choose that idea as well. What is the first step? Maybe you say that the work that you want to start needs to be done. Maybe you want to reach its last stop in your work, so you are going to start that work. Maybe you say that you want to start a certain work because after the completion of that work you will get a wonderful reward which you were imagining for a long time. You may say that my boss forces me to work that's why I am doing this work otherwise I would just go to my favourite destination. It is also possible that without doing this work how can I satisfy the customers of my business so that I can get a huge profit.

You can give any answer like reward, salary, benefits, restraint, this work is part of my regular life, this work is my child's desire, my wife will not come home if I don't fulfil her demand. I will sign the paper containing any reasons you give for starting any work.

If you sit and think calmly before starting any work of your life, then you must complete these two steps, without this the

chances of success of any work become very less.

First of all, you need to have a desire to do the work you are going to start.

This is a very important step that you need to consider but you don't. You use this step very lightly in your life. Whenever this step comes to you before starting any work, you have many excuses for it. Let's say, you get an offer from a company which is ready to give you a handsome salary which you can meet the essential needs of your life and also you get a short break from your job in the evening. Which you can also enjoy. But there is a condition attached with that job which you do not recognize at that time or you do not want to consider that condition which you have to fulfil before joining that job. This condition is not about the rules and regulations of the company or you have to sign some document in which there is a condition that you can not leave this company before one year in your job or there is something scary which you have to fulfil before joining that company.

No, I do not want to mention such words in the example of my book. Instead, I want to mention that you don't like the job but you like the salary that the company is ready to offer you. You don't want to do that company's assigned work because you don't like that work. You know this at the time of joining that job but what do you do that you give a long list of excuses to hide that thing and that to no one else, You tell yourself that excuse again and again. Like, I've been doing a job for a long time that didn't meet my financial needs, which is what this job can do. My kids are also growing with their demand. So I need to kill my will. Getting a job as per my wish is rare nowadays so how can I get that kind of job.

Suppose I have an opportunity to do the work that I want to do, which I like, but if that job cannot give me enough money to run my house, what will I do? So many excuses, I'm sorry, I'm telling them your excuses. May it be all the facts of your life. But think calmly that if you are not happy in your job then how can you expect yourself to be successful in that job.

Success does not mean that you will get rich very soon by doing any work which you do not enjoy but the salary of that work makes you happy. Success means getting a promotion, getting a better position in whatever job you are doing and getting that promotion, getting that better position, which is far better than your old office desk. What do you think about how you can achieve promotion in your job? Simple, you will need to do better work at your job today than you did yesterday. You have to improve your work performance to get a better position in your job.

How can you imagine that even if you are not enjoying your job you can do better in that job to achieve the dream of promotion in that job? It's not possible at all. I am not saying that if you are not enjoying any job then you will not be able to do that work but if you are not happy with your job then you are less likely to get a promotion in that work.

If you are not believing my words then you need to look around you where you work. Think about your office right now. Think about the people who got a promotion in your office. Think of the people who will soon get a luxury chair in that office. What's one thing all these people have in common that you haven't thought of? That is their desire for their work. All those people are happy doing their work and that too not because they all get big check or they will get a promotion by doing all this. No, They are happy doing their work for which they do not need any other reason to start their work.

What helps them to work hard for that work, they enjoy doing that work. Such people don't set any goal like I need to complete this work in any way because by its completion I can get my reward. If I don't get that reward, I will be the only unhappy person in this beautiful world.

If you say I talked to him. I worked with him. I don't feel like all those people like their work, instead, they just focus on the goal which they wanted to accomplish. Maybe you are right. How can I reject your views? Because you are the person who doesn't get promoted but work with people who got promoted in their job.

But it is not 100% true. Those people may not have felt the same way about their work in the early stages of their work as they feel now. In the initial days of their job, it should be possible that they did not like their work but after some time they got success in finding good things in their work, These people were getting bored at the beginning of their work.

You can try this method in your work also.

For example, one day you concluded that you don't deserve your job. You do not like your work but there is also one thing that you cannot get another job which you can replace with your current job. Because suppose you are getting your pleasure in the new job that has been offered to you, but that work cannot fulfil your financial needs. Now you have only one option, which is to recognize the beauty of your current work. That means trying to find the good things that are already included in your current boring job. All those good things will motivate you to do that work more energized than before.

For example, if you are working on computers in your offices such as programming or doing data entry, any work related to sitting at the computer. If you do not like this type of job and your heart wants some thrill, you can contact the marketing department in your company. You can request to your boss that I am not able to enjoy my current job but I can do my best in the marketing field, so you transfer me to the marketing department. Such small efforts for you can create a better environment for your job which you used to find boring earlier.

I suggested the marketing department because you will have to travel a lot in that area. Of course, they will not send you to a beautiful hill station or you to spend the night in Goa. But your company will send you to another boring company office to represent and market their products and services. Your company is on the right track, they are not wrong with their decision. But you need to make yourself smart like one day your company sends you to another city to market their product and services which they want to sell. You can make a perfect plan which can fulfil the goal of your company and also fulfil the goal of your heart. If you complete the work given by your company in the stipulated time, then after that you can travel to the city you went to. All you need to do is make a list of things that are great in the city your company sent you. You will need to prepare everything in advance. You can search on the net to see which are the best places you can go to after finishing your work. All these make your dream come true. Your company's goal has been achieved. You don't have to leave your job. You do not need to worry about any financial needs.

I am not saying that everyone's favourite job is to travel. You just sit calmly and think what are the points in my job which can motivate me to do my job. You have to find the good stuff in your work as I showed you a demo I mentioned above. Because every person who has got any kind of success in any work, he must have seen good things in his work, which would help him to get up early in the morning and go to work every day. Without this, you cannot move forward in life and any job, you will just keep working continuously at the same place from where you started.

If you are not able to enjoy your work, then whether it is any business or any job, you will get the same kind of salary or benefits for a long time. It is not only about your enjoyment of work, but also about getting success in that work. To achieve success in whatever work you are doing, you need to find the side of that desire.

And the second step which you should complete before starting any work is your capability.

I think you always take this step the wrong way whenever you need to think about it. Yes, ability implies doubt in your ability to do a task but you always use this method in a negative aspect. Like, Will, I will be successful in my life or not? how will my wife be? Will my children listen to me or not? I am talking about these questions which you regularly ask yourself to create a doubt system for yourself. So it is useless for you to doubt yourself. Because in such a situation you do not analyze any such capability which should you doubt yourself.

First of all, you need to analyze any function. Before starting any work, ask yourself these simple questions. Like, can I do this or not? If you think you can't do that, ask yourself why you can't. Just after getting the answer to the first question, you do not have to start doing that work or run away from that work. Just wait and think about the things you can't do in the work you want to do. After recognizing those things, you need to learn those things in your work that prevent you from doing that work. You will be ready to do any work after getting answers to various questions asked by yourself in the analysis time of that task. We just need to adopt analysis for any work.

> **"Ability isn't about getting depression from doubting yourself. Ability drives us to a system of analysts that gives you a real reason why you can or can't do your desired job."**

Oler

Summary of these two phases: desire and ability

If you are going to start a job, you first ask yourself if you desire to do this job. If not, don't do it. If you have a lot of excuses for this line, then find good things in your boring work that can help you in doing that boring work.

If you are going to do some work then ask yourself whether I am capable of doing that work or not. But not in a negative way in which you have to take depression pills. Think positively and calmly. Let us take one more example for this.

If any of your friends need money. He has disclosed his need to you. In this story, you have the kind of ability that you can give your friend as much money as he is asking from you. But you have no desire in it. It means if you give your money to your friend but your desire is disturbed by it. Your desire tells you over and over again that you don't need to help your friend. You can't sleep at night worrying about the money you lent. You call your friend every week and try to know the condition of your money and in return, you get an answer that increases your blood pressure. If you get into all these dilemmas by using your ability to pay, then you should not use your ability in this way because you do not have any desire in it.

And if we understand this example from the aspect of desire, Like you have full desire to give money to your friend but you cannot pay the money that your friend is asking from you. What will you do then? Will you sell your house to help your friend so that your friend may be helped but your family will be homeless? Would you like to help like this? Will you take a loan to help your friend at huge interest which you have to repay? If you are not able to repay that loan at the right time, then just as your friend is facing financial troubles today, in the same way, you and your family will be forced to face a financial crisis even if you have money in hand.

We can understand well from both these examples that how important is desire and the ability to do any work.

EIGHT

TWO FRIENDS, TWO GYMS AND TWO GYM TRAINERS.

Today it is necessary for you to pay attention to this story, whose song I am going to hum in a while. Because the lesson of this story has inspired me to write this article today. Otherwise, there is no dearth in the arrival of thoughts during the winter, but it has become a bit difficult to thread those thoughts into the homes of words.

Now you have to ask yourself a question that do you have any objection to the word gym and the activities done in the gym? I do not want to challenge your laziness, but this story is mainly related to the machines that tire the body and give pain ie gym.

If your mind has agreed to this question, then I start my interesting story.

In the days of youth, if you have enough money, that you can fulfil your life-related needs as well as fulfil your precious hobbies, then the matter of life is something else. Along with this, if the time becomes kind during the same youth, that means that the people of your family do so much money-earning work that you do not have to suffer from any worry related to money, then you have the golden opportunity to live your life to the fullest. There is an opportunity and it is this opportunity that is most dear and effective because at the increasing stages of age, worldly responsibilities become more and one's desires and the spirit of the body starts decreasing to live life to the fullest.

I do not want to break the morale of old people through these teachings but it is a fact of passing age in life. But it is also true that with the power of the mind this truth can also be disproved.

Now your mind must have started rebelling after reading these thoughts. Not because all these ideas do not match with the reality of life, but because your mind thought of rebelling because this author promised to tell an interesting story in the opening words of this article but it did like a "saint" Has started preaching life, youth and enthusiasm. Where is the story told?

So the story is that two friends have recently stepped on the threshold of youth. Those who have gone through the phase of their youth will realize that most of the youth and girls of youthful days give more emphasis on improving their physical appearance than creating good thoughts and a good future, and if we talk about this dark Kaliyuga period, then there has been a huge jump in the figures of external appearances. If you take the help of simple words, in today's era, attention is given to external beauty. Whether it is a person, an object or an idea that is well presented but its meaning is of no use to you.

These two friends also thought of doing the same thing as a young man, giving up in front of his hormones, preparing himself to enjoy worldly pleasures in a good way. For stylish hair, get your hair cut at the city's best and especially the barber who has the most crowds. Always looking for the best clothes, which are recognized as the youth of today's age by wearing, but only by having stylish hair and wearing fashionable clothes will not complete the task of creating outer beauty, rather, to make your body more attractive (not to stay healthy) think of going to the gym full of machines of today's most innovative technology.

Ways to find gyms.

These two friends also want to change their physical appearance, Seeing the attractive body of a hero of a film or a person full of fitness qualities recently, both of them also thought of going to a gym to make their body the same. But before walking on any path, a person always has to pass through two stages. If he goes out on the way without crossing these stages, then he gets a pile of regrets in the end, not the destination.

Those two stages come before doing any work. First, your willingness to do that work and second, your ability to do that work. After examining these two steps at your level and after concluding, you know completely whether you should do that work or not. These two friends also went through these phases and one of the two friends decided that I would go to the best gym. I want to make my body most attractive no matter how much money it takes, I am ready to pay all those expensive bills.

Before hearing another friend's decision, I thought that we should name them. For how long will you keep calling the first friend and the second friend. Keeping the name will also increase the interest in the story. So the one who does not give any attention to expensive bills in front of his body, his name will be "Raj" and whose decision is yet to be heard, his name will be "Bholu".

So Bholu declared this, I do not have to run after renewal. I just have to exercise with hard work and dedication. The gym should be in a normal form, the kind where there is no change in my body language on the first day and at the same time which is not intended to lighten my dear purse. Raj and Bholu are good friends, but it is here that their ability stage has chosen different exercise places for them.

Those who are experienced in the activities of a gym and who have the knowledge that by doing which exercise in a gym, lifting, holding, pulling which weight will have more effect on a person's body, and also knows that when, how much and how to do that exercise so that a person can use his time and energy properly in the body part which a person wants to make attractive and effective.

If you do not know these above-mentioned things, then any exercise you do in a gym will be like a low-level labourer working in a factory and such a worker who is not getting wages in return for work but is paying wages.

Making employment Or Looking for employment.

So these experience people have given an important message to all those people who are going to take their first step in a gym built in any corner of the world. It simply means that when a person is of earning age, he starts making employment or looking for employment for himself.

By **making employment** here, I mean that doing own business, in which even if you have done a basic study of education given in any normal school, even then that person can run any business, but unless there is a need for any special education to run that business, such as tiffin service business, in which you need to have knowledge related to food. The most important information in this should be that how is the food prepared? It may be that in the initial days of this business, your financial condition is not such that you can hire a cook on a special basis for cooking, then at that time, you will have to fulfil that responsibility and it may also happen that your financial condition is good, but someday due to personal reasons of your cook, he is not able to cook, then at that time, you will have to handle that work.

And now coming to the meaning of **looking for employment,** in which a person is looking for such a job, by working in that job, that person can earn enough money by the end of the month so that he can fulfil the basic needs of his life and at the same time It also expects from that job that with increasing time, the salary of his job also increases so that he can also fulfil his hobbies in life. But just as some conditions are always present with every work, in the same way for "job search" also some conditions have to be fulfilled by the interested person.

But before that you also have to understand that there are also two types of "job search" and sometimes both these types are needed in many jobs. The first type of employment, which is given based on your education. The employment in which you are selected for the work is based on your education and mental ability to do the work related to a particular subject. Another type of employment, in which your education has no meaning. Only your physical contribution is needed in that employment i.e. labour employment.

As you know that in today's era, the literacy rate of every country is increasing, which means that now people's thinking is to earn money based on their mental ability and not to burn their body in harsh sunlight. In doing tiring work, in which the arrival of money is also less.

(In all these things, I do not want to hurt any labouring person. I know very well that every work has its importance and the one who does it also matters)

So the purpose of all these employment-related things is that in jobs based on mental ability, you must present your certificate of education. Which is called Resumé in the language of a job. In which from your secondary education to a particular subject in which you are interested, it includes certificates of the teachings of its Bachelor, Master and some other important skills.

Now coming to the issue for which I was telling you employment texts till now. To present all these education-related certificates, you must get them from any school, institution or college. For which you will start from the low level of education i.e. with the knowledge of the letters of the languages and gradually you will be able to reach the higher level by clearing the classes of the low level of education. Only then will you be able to show all your certificates to get a job. So you must have come to know from this that to do a job done on a mental basis, you have to sacrifice a large part of your age. Then you become eligible for that job. Nothing happens in a day.

listen to these experiences people.

Similarly, before doing any exercise, you need to know its ABCD. Which exercise to do? How many times to do? What is the right position to do the exercise? If I am worried about my obesity, what exercise do I need to do to lose weight? And if I am lean, then which exercise do I need to pay more attention to? How much time do I need to spend in a gym to make my body the way I want? And most importantly, what kind of food do I need to eat after exercising? So that the hard work done by me gets the right results.

Like, to get an education, a good teacher is needed in an authentic school or in a special way. Similarly, for exercise-related education, a guru i.e. gym trainer is needed. Who can give you the correct answer to the above-mentioned questions?

No work is done without paying its due price.

Now answering all these exercise-related questions was a one-of-a-kind task. What a gym trainer does. If you have spent a considerable amount of time in this worldly life, then you must know that no work is done without paying its due price. Every work, every commodity or every service has a price, on the payment of which you can enjoy that commodity or service.

If we look at this world with only one eye, then we will get the conclusion that the price of any goods and services is only the official money of the country where we live. But we are not going to believe with a single glance. We have to understand this world closely so that we can live this worldly world in a better way. For which both eyes and ears have to be kept open, and to understand this world better, we have to keep our mouths open so that we can ask the right question to the right person, at the right time. This is the rule by which we can quickly solve worldly problems and many questions.

In the process of finding this solution, I want to tell you this important thing that, Money is not the only medium to be given always and everywhere in exchange for any goods and services. Many of you must have been a little surprised after reading this, but your surprise is going to end through this story.

As in the story of our two friends, Raj indulges in innovative technology gym machines and gives him an expensive bill in his hand every month, and as we also know through this story, Raj is born in the gym world in recent times. So it is clear from this that he may not have been at all familiar with the exercise activities done in a gym and to become familiar with those activities, he will need a guru i.e. a good gym trainer. What is the importance of a Guru, you must have understood from the above thoughts written by me and if any person, goods or service has importance in our eyes, then obviously it will have some value,

Only after paying, we will be able to take advantage of that goods or services. In today's modern age expensive gyms, there is no need to find a guru i.e. gym trainer. Whenever you take your first step in such a gym, while taking the membership of a gym, you are given a wonderful offer by the operator or manager of that gym to attract you, which you can never refuse. To entice you, they come up with an offer where you are shown a golden opportunity to get huge discounts on having a gym trainer with the gym. To refuse which your mind is already lost in front of their sweet sweet words.

I am in the gym, now which exercise should I try.

In this digital world, people who are in the early days of any gym, ask many more questions to YouTube and Google than taking the help of a living gym trainer, I am in the gym, now which exercise should I try. It is a very good step to increase one's knowledge about any subject, but it is also important to know the real purpose of the source giving that information. We are not living in any Satyug or Tretayug. Where we can blindly trust anyone for any work. If you have forgotten from the articles of good things written by me, then let me remind you that we are standing under the sky of dark Kaliyuga, not even Kaliyug. In which the rain of good does not rain according to the season but according to the kindness of nature.

If your memory is back, then let me keep in mind that every video you watch on YouTube and every page you click on Google is in "views counting". Understanding "views counting" in simple words, is a new dimension of doing business and marketing and is very influential with the existing businesses and marketing measures in the world. Google and YouTube are like a platform on which different types of creators present their dramas with their different specialities. To take full advantage of these dramas, big multinational companies are keen to get their products and services recognized in a big way or to remove the deficiency in the sales of their products and services, These companies appeal to forums like Google and YouTube to help us in spreading advertisements of our products and services to as many people as possible through the dramas displayed on your platform. In return for this assistance, companies pay a heavy price, in which they do not have any problem. These companies also have a complete idea that the money invested by us will not go in vain. Through those advertisements, we will earn double the value by selling our products and services.

Now from here comes the responsibility of forums like Google and YouTube, which choose the advertising of different types of products and services given by companies, among the dramas that are spread on their forums. For example, if a company wants to make the advertisement of its adornment item reach a large number of people, then according to this, YouTube and Google will find those dramas on their platform which are directly and indirectly related to the adornment.

And the surprising thing is that these dramas do not make by a platform like Google and YouTube. The full contribution of making these dramas, common man like you and me, who create these dramas by using their skill and mental power. What we get in exchange for these dramas, the meaning of "views counting" emerges from here. That is, those who make dramas, those creators do not get money immediately after making their dramas. According to the number of audiences who take part in the viewing of those dramas, their price is decided. That's why every day new types of dramas are seen for free but they are not free. The value of those dramas, we spend our time and at that time, if we are impressed on the advertisement displayed during that drama, then click on it or just see that advertisement, then understand that you have paid your price for watching that drama.

In this way, the triangle business and marketing cycle run in which the web of profit is woven. Very few creators can escape from this trap and whose only purpose is to reach their drama to the people, the drama of those creators is likely to be true. Otherwise, most of the creators come under the temptation of "view counting" and start making such plays, which more and more people see and which have nothing to do with truth and goodness. That's why I tried to wake you up through my words above that how you should exercise and what diet should be taken before and after exercising. Whether the person telling this priceless rule is trustworthy or not. After examining and testing it, you should proceed with your step.

The Currency of Respect.

Now we come to the characters of that strange story, the way the story is told, you will be in a lot of surprises you have never heard such a story before. So Raj was also listening to this story and taking inspiration from this story, instead of free gurus from Google and YouTube, he decided to take gym lessons from a living guru who was in front of him.

Bholu also took the same step and if we face the truth then as mentioned in our story Bholu had decided to sweat himself in a normal gym. So it is a matter of course that there is no hope of having such facilities in that gym which will make you feel like a five-star hotel and Bholu's gym was so simple that there weren't officially many trainers that Raj's gym had. As soon as you go to the gym, like a hotel, hand you a menu and ask you lovingly what is your physical goal? What type of body do you want? We have this list of different types of experienced and knowledgeable trainers that have captivating names as well as fixed prices. In which Raj has to choose a trainer of that price according to the capacity of his pocket for his exercise education.

There was only one trainer in Bholu's gym, who was also the caretaker of that gym, who was also the sweeper of that gym, along with a good capable trainer whose speciality was not kind to any paper. He used to express his speciality to the members joining that gym by the way of his learning.

The most important thing was that of Bholu's trainer, due to which we have been able to fix such a distance that Bholu's trainer does not charge his training fee in common currency in exchange for giving his effective training to the members involved in that gym. Rather, he used to take the price of feeling good in return for his training. That is respect, just nothing else.

In today's time, we have become so much mathematicians that we see any item or service or any good words or work done by any person by connecting it with the numbers of money. We calculate the data in our mind that this person did this work for me, now I will have to pay the value of money in such numbers.

No matter how much a person goes in modern times, no matter how mean he becomes, no matter how much evil prevails over good, but in the end, only good feelings will win because man cannot get rid of his emotions with the development of the mind. The feelings he got from being born as a human being. Emotions are also possessed by animals but they are not able to manage it properly because for doing the management the brain is needed which is with the human being.

What are good feelings, on feeling that, we start feeling very good on the inner side? Life is much better than before. We like it even if the weather is bad. We start looking for the good in people instead of the shortcomings. Overall, good feelings make us a good person and in bad feelings, we expose our bad form in front of people even if we do not want to.

If you look at the list of good feelings, love, appreciation, kindness, help, honesty, satisfaction, positive thinking and most importantly "respect" according to this article. You must have realized that whenever we go through all these good feelings, it does not matter whether you are supplying these feelings or fulfilling the demand. You will feel a good feeling in both the process. Your that moment, that time or maybe that whole day you spend in that good feeling. That too until you are faced with a new bad feeling.

Bholu's trainer wants these good feelings and especially the feeling of respect in return for his training. Because his financial need is fulfilled by the owner of that gym, but it does not mean that there is any pressure on him from his owner that you will train the gym members along with handling the gym. If he wanted, he could also pass the time on video games by sitting in a corner. But he thought of imparting proper exercise knowledge to his gym members, that too free of cost. But not without respect.

Raj was also working hard as a labourer in the gym and Bholu was also engaged in making a good body by doing his labour. The trainers of both were giving their gym knowledge and experience to these two newborn creatures. The only difference was that Raj's trainer waits for green notes on the last date of every month and Bholu's trainer expects only respect from Bholu every day.

It is a process of respecting that trainer.

To understand this chapter more closely, we have to understand what is the meaning of respect? Is it an honour to invite a person to your home for hospitality? Is it respectful to ask a friend about his and his family's well being? Is it respectful to have human moral values with a person?

Respect includes all these things, but many important things are lacking in them. listening to a person's point of view, then understanding the words spoken by him and then you have to make him understand your point and his mistake.

It is a process of respecting that trainer. Bholu's trainer also wants Bholu that he should listen to him, do the exercise he is telling, do it in the way he has been told. Don't put your mind. Ask your trainer to do each exercise and after doing each of the mentioned exercises, ask the question "which exercise should I do next". Come to the gym on time and give as much time as the gym trainer is asking for to do the exercises that tire your body. Eat whatever the trainer has told you to eat regularly and do not even think about what he has told you not to eat. **This is the process of listening to that gym trainer.**

Now understand these things very well and after that, the exercise which you are facing difficulty in doing or if there is any injury in any part of the body, then share that thing with your trainer. **This is the process of understanding that gym trainer.**

It's just respect. This is how Bholu's trainer wants his money.

Raj's trainer has nothing to do with this kind of respect. He only needs the respect of money at the end of the month. Raj's trainer gives him knowledge and experience related to exercise, but if Raj does not follow that knowledge, then Raj's trainer does not have any problem as Bholu's trainer. Now it is the responsibility of Raj further whether he should follow those things or not.

Even in ordinary life, there are many such works, which sometimes need to be respected for getting them done, which can be false or true. Hospitality (Respect) or Bholu's trainer (Respect) Sometimes, in many things, work is done only with money. Just as it is necessary to have money in the pocket to buy soap, no matter how well you deal with the shopkeeper, he will not give you soap for free, and sometimes it is necessary to have both aspects.

NINE

IS IT BETTER TO HELP SOME PEOPLE A LOT OR HELP A LOT OF PEOPLE A LITTLE?

During my school days, I was accustomed to always hearing this message from the teachers during the examination that "After reading every question thoroughly, understanding it, and after that then writing your answer." Then in childhood mischief did not pay attention to that precious message, but today as soon as this question comes to the fore, the message of the teachers is well understood.

After reading this question too, you directly followed his "words" and set out to fulfill the purpose of those "words". As the word "help" has been mentioned in this question and other words have also been included, then only that sentence is made so that a question can be formed. So that we can answer that question and not some "words" of that question. At first, you focused only on the word "Help" and from beginning to end your gaze was on that word and the result was that your answer is completely devoted to that one word and not to the question asked. If in this way we try our perspective on every question that comes in life, then life will pass but we will not be able to fulfill the duty of that human life.

Our problem is that whenever we do some good work, we just do that work without any scale and congratulate ourselves, what work have I done today. But we do not stop for a while and think that how much good is being done by doing that good work of mine, for how long my good work will be with those people with whom I have shown my goodness and if only for a short time, This good work will be with those people, so what should I do so that they remember my goodness for a long time, it will be useful for them.

It would be completely wrong to answer this question on numbers or scales because it does not matter how many people you are helping or how much you are helping. Instead, how is it helping? That is all that matters because it is a good thing for you to arrange one meal for someone. But the even better thing would be that that person should sit on someone else's trust to satisfy his hunger instead he should be capable that he does not have to wait for you to satisfy his hunger.

That is, you should find such employment for him according to his skill, education, and choice, which will not only benefit him, but he can spend his family's whole life without any mercy from the salary received from his employment.

In this type of help, you do not have to think about how much you have to help or how many people to help because it does not matter until you think about how to help. So that once you give help, the person seeking help never needs to seek help in life.

The exception is present everywhere, it means that in every good place, in every good deed, in every good thought and every good feeling, exception runs from the beginning. In which exception is like a possibility which warns or misleads you. Say anything in both, but the bad form of every action, thought, and feeling initiated by you tells you along with its good form. But the matter then comes to the same exception, in which the issue of attitude is also included, how do you look at them? Similarly, if a person is unable to work or does not want to work, then he will be in search of mercy again.

TEN

HAVE YOU FORGOTTEN YOUR PURPOSE?

What is the first thing you do when you wake up in the morning? Please do not include those things in your answer, the things that we like to say and at the same time we also want to adopt those things in our life but they are related to real-life to some extent. Every article I write is written to help you in some way or the other, so how can I forget the conveniences in this chapter, by which you will be able to understand my thoughts even better.

By convenience, I mean those examples that by adapting a real situation into a fictional story, we can easily acquire the knowledge of a subject matter by adopting a real situation into a fictional story.

The things that I am requesting you not to use in your answer are such as, I do exercise first thing in the morning. I wake up in the morning, first of all, I thank the creator of this world for allowing me to take birth in a human body on this earth. I touch the feet of my parents.

There are many other courteous person related sentences that I can use in this example system, but I am sure you must have understood what I request you not to use in the answer to my question. If we take a look towards the mirror of truth, to find the answer to this particular question, then we will find that in this modern age where we are using different types of technology as our convenience, instead of using them as our convenience, we have made them an integral part of our life. Out of these integral parts, I want to mention that important part i.e. that technology in this chapter, which we used to call a phone a few years ago and as our needs start increasing from that phone device, then we have adopted its technology form and changed according to our convenience and the name of calling it also changed, which we call smartphone in today's era.

This is that object, if we get the surface of the outer shell examined scientifically, then we will undoubtedly get such a conclusion, which we should not be surprised at all. Because from this conclusion we will know that our fingerprints will be found on our beloved smartphone which will be many times more than anything we touch in this world, whose count may be non-numeric.

In the examples, I used to make you understand the courteous things I mentioned. Do not disturb your mind by reading those examples. Perhaps many of you readers would have done such courteous acts as soon as the first ray of the sun came out. But my question here is, what is the first thing you do in the morning? Not that I asked, what do you do when you wake up in the morning? And the answer to this question will surely be that, in this extreme modern age, most of us give our precious time to our smartphone, which is more important than our body part, immediately after the completion of the last moments of our sleep.

Many of you readers must be thinking that today's chapter, what is it about, how we should use our smartphone in a useful way? Then I should read something more useful soon because I know very well how to use my smartphone. I don't need any special knowledge for this.

Yes, your opinion may be right in this matter, but today the matter is different. What I mean to say is that I am not going to give any guidelines regarding how to use a smartphone correctly, rather I want to share with you an anecdote related to my smartphone through this chapter and you know that every chapter written by me narrates useful messages in life.

I would like to add this anecdote to this series of useful life messages, which was started by my best friend and came under my observation through my smartphone. Without wasting your time, I will directly tell you the merits of that incident.

As you know, in this modern era, the phone is not used only for important conversations. In the old times, one rupee had the opportunity to talk for only one minute and with every minute increasing our liver used to come out too. Today where we take the whole world with us with our phones. Whenever anyone, sitting in any corner of the world, not only do we listen to his voice, but also establish such a conversation with him, as if he is in front of us.

In the old times, if we had to meet someone, discuss with someone, inquire about someone's condition and have any kind of contact, then we immediately go to the place of residence of that person, no matter how far that place travels. Yes, we would have crossed that distance on the strength of our will and ability. But now that kind of problems do not exist and yes, it can be said that the form of problems has changed with the increasing time.

It is not only about our modern smartphone, but every single device present in today's time is our increasing need or it would be correct to say that, to make even the smallest tasks easier by us, we are constantly looking for new technologies. In the case of these modern technologies, I have unique strange thinking, which you may find strange after reading it, but somewhere we are trying every day to implement this unique strange thinking.

The title of this strange thought of mine is magic. Yes, magic. You must have read, heard the word, the interesting, fictional, mythological stories associated with it and especially since the advent of television, we have all seen movies promising to uncover the world of magic. If you have ever studied stories or real events related to a magic subject through listening, watching and reading, then you must have noticed one thing that whoever is a magician, he does him every work, whether that work be it small or big, whether that task is difficult or easy and no matter how long the time is in that task, that magician utters a mantra to it in a pinch or by adding words we have never heard in life. Or by rotating a golden attractive stick, it does all its work in an instant which is impossible for a normal person to do.

We are also trying to implement this "one-moment" sentence every day in today's time through different and unique efforts. Today we are also doing the same magic with the medium of our modern technology. In magic stories, how a person had to have any kind of conversation with another person, then that person would do magic and suddenly appeared in front of that interested person. We are also doing such unique work in today's era. Whenever we felt like, we exposed the words immersed in the depth of our heart to anyone, that too in a moment through video calling technology, in which we not only hear the voice of that person but also we take a look at the face of that person along with his or her clothes and many more works that we see are done by magic in magic stories, today we are doing those same tasks with the help of technology like magic or even more effectively than magic.

Whether we give the name of magic to today's technology or call it a feature that makes tasks easy or a scientific name to be kept by the discoverer, it will not make any difference in the working of that technology.

The difference is not in the name but for what purpose we use that scientific facility, the difference is in that matter. To introduce you to this difference, let me tell you an anecdote of my friend, which is based on this entire chapter.

One day my best friend through the WhatsApp application present inside his smartphone (whose information will be like a joke, because all of you have used this application a lot and the story I am going to mention, you have participated in that event many times.) Sent a life useful message on the status that those words were not said by my friend but by some great man. You must think that it is good that your best friend is sending a positive message to people. Your friend has made good use of this WhatsApp technology, what's wrong with it? There is nothing wrong, but an act has happened which my friend is not aware of and when you also do such actions, you are also oblivious to this realization, which you will know after a while till the last word in this chapter.

That feeling is that whenever my friend or any person among you spreads a life useful message to the people in this way or through any social media, whether that message is given by a great man or any person himself, written by his intellect's ability. By reading any such message, we get a new direction of life, by reading that message, we find a way out by which we can get out of the immediate troubles of our life, immediately after reading that type of message, we would have such a feeling. It is that we should tell this message to those who know us. But, but, but, while doing actions in this way, our aim is not that this message will benefit the people of my acquaintance, this message will show them such a path in their life that will save their life and at that time it is not even a purpose that I will appear as an intelligent person among my friends, relatives and those who know me. So that you do not feel bad, I can say that the quantity of these two can be to some extent, but our real purpose in all this is that

> *"The things, the rules and the thoughts of different types of great men, We want to adopt those ideas with great passion in our life but we get more happiness in shouting those things to the people around us, especially to the people connected with us on the devices of social media, Instead of focusing on those words, which have given us a new life. "*

And you must have heard this statement which makes our life easier many times in your life that we should always do one task at a time, which increases the chances of completing that task effectively. This invaluable statement supports the chapter I wrote today, because whenever we send a pleasing message through social media, whether it is written by any particular person, which we have read at any time, At the same time, we take the responsibility of taking that message to the people in our hands.

In all this, our main purpose of reading that useful message ends at the same time which was that we have to conduct the words written in that message. Try to follow the things and rules mentioned in it. We have to think about walking on the paths which have been shown.

Now after reading this chapter, many of my readers must have started evaluating me based on what I have told them "This writer is also doing the same work. No no no, My thoughts do not let me sleep, so I reach you, people, through my blog website, through my books. That type of rule will not apply here, the type of rules or things I have mentioned in this chapter. Because in any message you send, you mostly want to bring that message into your life, but instead, you tell people what you read today. While I try to write the experiences I got in my life on my blog website, on my books, with a useful life message. So that I want you to get some kind of help through my words.

It is also not my intention that I am humiliating you and presenting myself as God. What I mean to say is that most people while sending life useful messages on social media get involved in the activities mentioned this chapter, wanting or not wanting.

ELEVEN

HOW TO TOLERATE THIS NALLA (USELESS PERSON) WORD?

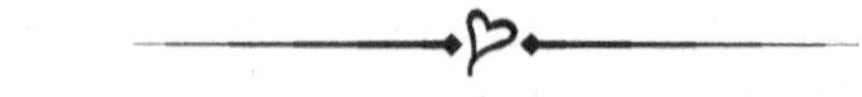

NALLA (Useless Person) is a word that is generally used in the streets of India for those people who are of no use to the person. Which is free all day. Keeps breaking free bread. Overall, such a person whose age has become worth earning, even then he depends on his family for his living. So to harass such a person, to make fun of him, everyone gets a chance to call him Nalla.

But one thing is clear from this that it will hurt anyone. Perhaps your intention is not to hurt that person's heart. You may have used this word only to convert the atmosphere of that time into laughter or you intend to hurt that person by calling him Nalla. You can give any excuse, but your using such a word for him will make that person feel bad. It may be that when you have called him Nalla, then at that time that person has pretended not to feel bad, but he has thought a lot about this behaviour of yours after going to his house. This might be possible.

You can also say that he is my best friend. I can call it anything. My friend will never mind my words. Maybe it could be. This is your idea. But have you ever tried to know from your friend, do you feel bad when I say you are Nalla?

Now I ask you the question that have you ever asked this kind of worrying question to your friend? You keep saying big things to your friends that you are my best friend. I can do anything for you. Which girl do you like, I go and tell her about your heart. It is good that you say things that strengthen your friendship and do such things so that your friend can trust you blindly. But caring for a friend is also a part of friendship.

The concern should not be only on the upper end. One should be concerned with the real issues, like trying to know the reason from him, why is he free?

- Why is your friend not doing anything?
- Why is your friend bringing such a situation that you have to call him Nalla?
- Is your friend not getting the job he likes? That's why he is sitting unemployed at home?
- If he's got his favourite job, why isn't he starting it?
- If there is any problem in starting that work and you can remove the problem of your friend with your ability and desire, then you should remove that problem.

Just calling your friend Nalla Nalla in the name of friendship and making fun of him is not friendship, but knowing the real reason for his indifference and removing that reason is friendship and then you can truly say anything to your friend. You can have the right. Even if you are calling him Nalla, it will work.

Now we have come to know what this Nalla word means and how bad your friend feels by using it. But till now we have not known the real purpose of writing this article.

So let us come to the real issue of our article that How to tolerate this NALLA word?

India is such a country where the solution of everything is found before its creation. Whether it is a law or such a bad idea. The people here have solved everything. The people here know what to handle and how. Same if you are free. Apart from eating and sleeping in your life, you do not do any work to earn money and you also want that people who know you should not make fun of you and even if they make fun of you, there is hidden respect in it, then you are welcome in this article. Because here you will be given such a trick, so that even if someone calls you Nalla, you will not feel bad and if you are stuck in a situation where you have to introduce yourself, that too without making fun of yourself, then up use this trick. You will be able to introduce yourself without any hesitation. And one more interesting thing is that you know this trick but maybe you have never used it.

"So without any delay, the name of that trick is a government job."

Yes, you've got it right. If you are not doing any work in your life, especially such a work that people consider you responsible and from which you get a fixed income. If you are not able to do this work for some reason. The reason could be anything.

- Maybe you are not getting your purpose.
- Perhaps instead of the work you are interested in, your well-wishers are pushing you towards the work that you do not want to do, so you are not doing anything now.
- Perhaps the work you want to start, there are some obstacles in starting the work, such as due to financial constraints.

The reason can be anything but the real thing is that you are in that situation right now where your well-wishers are looking for a chance to call you Nalla. Which opportunity you do not want to give at any cost. **For this, all you have to do is that whenever people try to know about your daily routine or ask you what work you do, instead of "I do nothing", "I am preparing for a government job" just Say this in your answer.**

It does not matter whether you are preparing for any government job or not. No one is going to come to your house to see you whether you are studying properly or breaking the clock. Yes, after reading this you can say that it is a lie. Yes, it may or may not be. Because I have seen so many people who have been giving the same answer for many years whenever people ask them what you do. I am not saying that all those who say so, prepare for government jobs, they do not. Maybe most of them are preparing for any government exam.

The exam of a government job,

is not such that you will be selected as soon as you fill the application form for that exam. This is just the first step to giving that exam. To pass that exam, you have to study many times better than those who are giving the exam and it is also important to remember what you read in that exam hall at the right time.

I don't even mean to say that those whose government exam is not clear, all of them were lying. No, rather it gives an idea that whenever people ask you what you do and you do not have any such answer which can make them understand that I am not doing any work right now because the purpose of my life is some other way in which I am searching but recently I am unemployed and free. If you tell your real situation to the people that you are unemployed and free and with that you give any strong reason to them, even then people will not hold back from making fun of you. Your well-wishers will try to taunt you in different ways. Will make you feel bad as if you have committed some sin.

You will come to that situation where you will not like to meet people because wherever you go, you have to introduce yourself in some way or the other.

- Even if you go with your group of friends,
- Even if you go to the function of a relative,
- Even if you are at your home and suddenly a neighbour comes to visit you.

So all these people will not be able to live without asking you about your work because it is their birthright. With this, these people try to identify and create a status so that these people want to know from you whether they should sit with you or not. Whether these people should have any kind of relationship with you or not. If you give such an answer in return, "I am preparing for a government job", these people will not ask you any work-related question after this, because these people shine as soon as they hear the name of the government job. These people feel proud of you. Appreciate you because you chose the path of doing a government job.

If you do not know the importance of a government job then you will never understand why I am putting so much emphasis on the pretext of a government job.

On a special note, government jobs in India have a different status. Not only after getting that job, but a happy atmosphere starts as soon as any government job form is filled.

- People have respect for you in their hearts, who till now considered you unemployed and worthless.
- People start talking to you well.
- People try to know your opinion on every issue on which till now you were kept sidelined.

But what is it like in a government job that has such an atmosphere of it?

Government job means you become free from financial worries for life because you would have known that every month my heart-pleasing salary will come in my bank account and every year without any extraordinary work my salary will keep increasing. Whether I do my work honestly or not in that job, it doesn't matter to me, I know this thing that no one can remove me from this job. Yes, maybe a citizen of this country will be dissatisfied with my work and complain against me, but what will happen to me, more and more I will be transferred but no one will be able to remove me from my job, so much I believe in my government job. My government job is not like a private company job, in which even after the work time is over, my boss will continue to work on me. No, once I come home from in government job, after that there is no worry related to my job work, I will do my favourite work in life with ease. And how many benefits can I count on doing a government job in a country like India? Coming home early from work, government job lunchtime is increased from the normal lunchtime, or it is made bigger intentionally. After retirement, you get such a huge amount that you can live the life of your two births with that money and not only this, even after getting that big amount, you get half of the salary you had at the time of your work under the government pension scheme. It is given to you every month after your retirement and given to your wife after your death so that she does not miss you financially after you leave.

Now, what more do you need from any work where you do not have any pressure to work, whatever your expenses in life, you get double your money, people around you start respecting you more than any common person. You can sleep peacefully at night. Overall, doing any government job and just filling the exam form of any government job can save you from the taunts of people.

I am not saying that you do not have to do any work by lying like this and just keep sleeping throughout the day. No, if that's your purpose then you are doing a lot wrong with your life and your family's expectations. The excuse of preparing for a government job is for those people who want to do something in their life, but for the time being, they are facing some problem in starting their work, because of which they are sitting free now or it would be more correct to say that this kind of work People are still engaged in thinking. Once they find a way to start their desired work, these people will not stop.

Such an excuse for such people can save them from the taunts of well-wishers, from making fun of themselves, from their heart-wrenching words. People will not bother you with this excuse and you will also make a good plan to start your work under the guise of this excuse. And at the same time, you will also be able to live your normal life, which till now you were running away from people because of your unemployment.

I want to tell you again this important thing that this excuse is only for those people who want to do some work in their life but they do not understand anything right now, so such people are still free. But these people also want to avoid being made fun of by well-wishers, then under the guise of this excuse, especially in a country like India, unemployed and free, they can avoid being made fun of by well-wishers.

Now no one will call you NALLA. While introducing yourself "I am preparing for a government job. Game finish, you will be able to live your normal life.

TWELVE

WHAT CAN I DO WITH THIS PAIN?

Misery is a situation from which everyone wants to run away, but can not run away even if they want to. Have you ever thought that what is the reason that misery comes into your life due to some reason or the other? It may be that there may be a decrease or an excess in its quantity, but suffering does come. The amount of suffering in your life is less and more, it depends on how much importance you give to your sorrow or it can also be said how important that sadness is to you. Just like losing a Rs 100 note from your pocket might not be as painful for you as someone running away with your expensive Apple iPhone out of your hands. It is not just about the money that with your Rs 100 note, you have lost only Rs 100. But the loss of your iPhone from your life is a loss of lakhs of rupees. Your importance to your suffering is not money but from that money or any person or any work or any emotion or your pet or your success or any of your favourite thing or someone's answer, Or how much emotional attachment you have with all your expectations towards your life, the more you will be sad when it comes to its negative consequences. The more attachment you have to whatever part of your life, the sadder you will be to see its negative face.

Based on this, an example can be that one day you get the news of a distant relative of yours leaving this world and on the same day, your pet cat who has been lovingly brought up by you for a long time passes away.

Now the outcome of your trial of suffering will depend on your emotional attachment. If your emotional attachment is less attached to that distant relative, then you will not feel as sad at the loss of that relative as you would be saddened by the loss of your cat. Because there was a great expansion in the range of your emotional attachment, whose misery is not for everyone to understand.

That's why having some kind of positive expectation from anyone at all times becomes a source of misery for you. Yes, it can bring happiness too. A possibility is there for both, only thinking good does not make good, for that one has to work hard to get that good by making a good strategy. The result of which depends on your hard work, your strategy and your external situation. You can control your hard work and strategy, but you do not have control over the external situation. So the result of every result can be positive or negative. Which means you can get happiness or sadness.

The best example to understand this is that you express your love to a person. In your way, you have truly loved that person. You have spent many days and nights in loving memories of that person. You have tried to do everything that will make that person happy and in this atmosphere of love, you spoke your love words to that person on a beautiful day. now what? Now from here, you have lost your control. Now it is the turn of that person to answer your love for you. The result of that answer will not be entirely on your true heart, rather it will result in the likes and dislikes of that person. His answer will be on the current status of that person. The answer will lie in that person's outlook on the future. Overall, if you find the answer in simple words, then you will find that that person must have the same feeling of love towards you like the feeling of love is present in you. If he is also flowing in the same spirit of love then it is fine. But if not, then that person will answer you in love with "No".

But the logic of your mind should be here that if suffering is as true as happiness then why do I always run away from misery?

You should ask such questions. Just by looking at life with wonder and by accepting whatever life is giving you without thinking, then you can enjoy the wonder you get every day. But you may find it difficult to live the same life in a better way. If you want to live life better then you should spend your time in knowing life, and in knowing that your knowledge should be focused on truth. Who can tell you what is the real truth of life and what was your illusion till now?

If you try to examine the subject of sorrow in this link of truth and illusion, then you will know that sorrow does not come again and again in your life, but happiness comes and goes again and again. Grief is always with you, it just keeps on changing in its form. But sometimes you feel happiness. Because you are always in search of it, thinking that this time if I get this happiness, then I will be happy forever. But this doesn't happen. Once you fulfil any of your wishes, you are happy for a short time, but after that, you get bored with that happiness and then after that boredom state of sadness comes into your life. To overcome this, you make goals of getting new happiness in your life. Then you start focusing on your hard work, time, strategy to achieve those goals. If every experiment you try while achieving that goal is according to your mind, then you are excited while achieving that goal, and because of that enthusiasm, you will be happy on the way to that hard work. But if your experiments show adversity, then you remain unhappy on the way to attain that happiness and you become unhappy all the time thinking about the goal of that happiness.

So the essence of all these things is that happiness is your guest and sorrow is your family member. With whom you always have to live and if you have already known that your sorrow is a member of your family, then learn to live with him, not run away from him. The farther you run, the more that misery will scare you and when it comes true it will give you a lot of pain.

Therefore, digest the truth, but it does not mean that after knowing this truth, you should not show any participation in achieving any desire in your life. My words do not mean that. You have to move forward, just keep the truth along with your expectations, so that you do not fall so much in the worst situation that you will find it difficult to come back.

It may be that by writing like this, your question will be on my side, whether I follow these rules or not. Yes, it is right, it is very easy for me to write in this way, but to follow the same written things is like climbing the highest mountain. But you have to start and it will have to be started with small steps because you cannot realize these useful things in a day. These will have to be included in the experiments of living your life every day. Only then will you be able to stand yourself in the greatest of sorrows.

So with so many discussions, it is proved that everyone has his sorrow, so this shows the truth that everyone is unhappy. Yes, the reason for everyone's sadness is different and there can be a difference in their quantity, depending on the importance they give to their suffering.

But the question is not whether you are sad or not? Rather, your question should be that what can you do in your sad situation or what do you do in real terms?

If your emotional attachment is to a lesser extent in the state of your sadness, then you work to hide that sadness. This means that you do not pay that much attention to your suffering or you do not want to give it. So in a situation where your emotional attachment to your suffering is less. You are not giving that much importance to the misery so that you can divert your attention from your normal life activities. Then you do these two things in a situation of less importance to your suffering.

1. Pretend to be happy by hiding your sadness.

Who would be such a person, who would hide his sorrow and pretend to be happy? Simply put, a person whose life is caused by the loss of his person or any other kind of loss or loss of any valuable thing, Or the damage that has not affected the person physically, mentally and emotionally so much that due to which that person feels any special upheaval while living his daily life. So in such a situation, this form of this person cannot be called a pretence to hide his sorrow, but if you try to put it in simple words, then that person has not been hurt a lot by that harmful incident in his life. Seeing whom everyone will say that this person is not sad.

Because how can you recognize the suffering of a person? Unless that person expresses his grief as clearly through his gestures, then you cannot use your common sense to tell whether this person is sad or not? No emotion has been expressed by any means and you can't fulfil the responsibility of testing it while keeping it in normal condition. Unless you use your understanding to a particular level, to identify his latent feeling on that person. Therefore, for any sorrow that has come in a person's life, it is necessary to express that sad feeling through the gesture of that person, so that the people who meet him can decide only after seeing him, that this person is unhappy.

But then after coming to this notion, your question should be that does a person never pretend to be happy and hide his sadness? No, pretends. When a person is faced with these parts of his life while living in his misery.

The parts which are included.

1. Greed
2. Fear
3. Any significant responsibility
4. Authority
5. Indulge yourself in your favourite work.

To satisfy some kind of greed, if a person's misery binds him, then that person will keep on pretending to forget that sorrow or to be falsely happy until the greed thought by him is achieved.

Suppose your only sister is getting married. Which means you have a huge responsibility on your shoulders to accomplish all the work of his marriage effectively. With this, this is the first such occasion for your family, where you can rightfully call this occasion your festival. Because getting married in a house is bigger than any special festival. In which each member of the family with heavy energy and all the close relatives of that family want to attend that marriage. Everyone is already very happy two months before the wedding. Everyone in their way has started seeing their dreams of having fun in that wedding program. New clothes, the smell of sweets, trying to please the angry members of the family with fun and being happy with the tiredness of doing all the preparations for the wedding, is a different level of joy.

And amid these blissful moments, you who are the bride's brother comes to know about the wretched news that you cannot attend that wedding from the day of the opening ceremony to the day of the last event. Because in those days you have a special and important career role-playing examinations are organized. In which your presence is very important.

Now try to imagine this situation, where on one hand you are going to have important exams deciding life ahead and on the other hand your only sister is getting married in which you have an important responsibility, and you will never be able to get the joy you get from that marriage in future. So in such a situation will you turn away from that exam? No, but even if you want, your family will never agree that you play with your future life. They will insist on giving you those exams diligently even when you say no and you will have to obey their orders hidden in that emphasis.

So, when you are giving those exams, will you give your full attention to the misery that you have got due to not attending the wedding of your only sister or will you give all your attention to writing the answers to the questions in your examination?

It is obvious that you will suppress all your sorrows at that time and you will not be happy, but instead of that sorrow, you will concentrate all your attention on your responsibility of giving those exams well. You will forget all your sorrows even if you do not want at that time.

- And with this fictional story, you can also see your greedy part, which is hidden in your future better career.
- And from this fictional story, you can also guess the fear part of you, in which you will not have a good career in your life because of not giving those exams.
- And from this imaginary story, you can see that part of your responsibility, which becomes your ultimate duty to pass these exams with a good result and give a good position in your life, on which you and your family will later be To be proud.
- And based on this fictional story, you can also recognize the authority part, which your family shows on you when you choose your sister's marriage instead of going for that test.
- And if you change the imagination of this story from your other imagination, that is, you like to study and take part in examinations so much that you want to live the days of your examinations despite the marriage of your only sister.

But with all these fantasies, you also have to keep in mind that exceptions also exist with them, And the one exception is that if a person does not have that level of emotional attachment to his suffering, then his face can tell whether this person is sad or not. That is, there is a possibility of being unhappy in a person's life, there is also a possibility of being happy and there is also the possibility of forgetting that misery by doing things that complicate oneself.

2. A person goes to that moment, where he forgets his sorrow.

Here, the state of sadness brought by a person in his life does not only mean that that person is not attached to that level of emotional attachment, due to which he should not face any problem in forgetting or suppressing his sorrow. It may be that his sadness, has had an emotional impact on him to a great extent. It may be that whatever loss that person has felt in his life, the result of that loss is associated with that person's very emotional attachment. Which means that the person is very sad. The way he used to behave in his normal life, there has been a lot of change in his behaviour because of his sorrow. So much so that he is not able to give his necessary attention even to the important things related to his life. Now such a situation has come that most of his time is spent in some dark corner of his house. He had stopped meeting people from outside, now he has stopped talking to his family members as well. When a person deliberately thinks of being alone even though he is not alone, then understand that this life has not been life for him recently.

So does such a person always remain in such a situation, who does not feel any kind of good hope in his life. Who always lives in sadness. For whom suffering becomes so important that in front of it, he even distances himself from his sleep.

Now you think that who would want to be in such a situation forever? Always what, no one wants to feel such a dreadful situation even for a moment. So in the same way such an unhappy person is always looking for happy days for himself. He also wants that by any means his misery should end completely. Because his pain is not less than any physical pain. Research of science even says that the amount of pain we feel due to any physical injury, we get twice as much pain from emotional injury. Therefore, its timely treatment is more important than the treatment of any physical injury.

In case of any kind of minor physical injury, then through the primary treatment and through the immunity of your body, the wound of that injury gets healed over time. But the wound of a hurt, which is very emotionally important for a person, if it does not get the right treatment on time or a piece of good advice is not given then that suffering can get worse. After that, even if your whole body is physically healthy, you will internally consider yourself to be the sickest person in the world. It is the same as if a person's hand is chopped off, even then that person forgets that shortcoming with time and starts living a life of comfort. But a serious emotional injury to a person, which does not look so serious on the outside, has negative consequences for that person's entire body language and life ahead.

So in the hour of such despair, either that person himself starts looking for the paths on which he walks so that he forgets his sorrow for a while or else the good well-wishers of that person find that kind of entertainment and work means for him so that that person spends more of his time in completing those works, rather than thinking about his misery and keep getting sad.

Overall, you can call it the method of entanglement or forgetting your sorrow. The means of which a person can choose according to his mind, but whose goal is the same, to indulge himself in such works to lift himself from his misery, So that sorrow is not remembered at the time of that work.

Instead of giving you too many examples here on this notion, I would sincerely urge you to read that book, which will help you find the means to relieve your suffering in the true sense. That is "How To Stop Worrying And Start Living" by Dale Carnegie.

In this book, there are so many ways that you can use every remedy, lift yourself from your misery and get out of all your worries in a pinch, and if you do not have any kind of deep sorrow now, then you can read it to understand life better. Because life is like a cycle, in which the number of sorrows comes more often.

There is a sensible person above all these thoughts of sorrows.

After reading this, do not get immersed in the thought that I am a sensible person or not? If I had been a sensible person, I would not have suffered any kind of pain. Do not think so at all, because no matter how much intelligence a person is born with or he has earned that highest intelligence through his efforts in this life, he will still have to go through a state of misery. The only difference may be that his way of fighting his sorrows and appearing in front of people is different. Because of that different way, that person is called wise.

So what is that way?

1. A sensible person always introduces these three people to his troubles and sorrows.

So what is the first question that comes to your mind in any problem? That, Who can solve my problem? This is the most important question for everyone who has any kind of problem. Yes, whenever you are stuck in any problem you ask yourself who can solve this problem?

- How can it be solved?
- How many difficulties do I have to face while solving the problem?
- How much time will be consumed for the problem?
- Can I solve the problem myself?
- Or do I need the help of somebody who can help me to solve the problem?

Many more questions are rolling in your mind but the most important question is who can solve this problem when you are not able to solve your problem or you have less knowledge about that problem which you are stuck in, so you try to find such people who can solve your problem and make you free from your difficulties.

But the original difficulties start now,

When you search for such people who can solve your problem. Because, in this searching period you tell your problem to everyone who comes to you, without thinking that they can solve your problem or not. For instance, You have a problem with medical terms. You want to solve your medical issue and want to live free from such disease. Let's ask a question from yourself: who can solve this problem? A doctor who specializes in such a field which disease you have got. Correct.

Suppose you have a medical issue regarding your intimate parts, so you need a doctor who has the expertise and ability to solve your problem, Right. But you discussed your medical issue with everyone like your friends, your neighbours, your well-wishers, all those people whom you think that they all pray for you well, but the truth is, they all are not praying for you well only a few of them may be and remain maybe make fun of you. In a few days, you realize that most of them are making jokes at you about your medical issue.

- Some of them laugh at you, whom you tell the story of your medical condition with believing that they are your well-wishers.
- Some of them make memes about you.
- Some of them acclamation of looser tags about you in your area, in your city.

So now what will be your next step, Who do you think is to blame for what happened to you? You blame the people whom you told your story and they made jokes at you. But the real sense above circumstance happened with you because of you only, no one fault, it is only your fault who couldn't recognize the right people to tell.

Now the process of identifying the right people for your solution to a problem.

In life you have to face uncountable problems, the difficulty is not that you have a problem but the difficulty is that whom to tell which to you can free from your problem. You without thinking about this and ask everybody who crosses near you. This is not the right approach to solve any problem, in reverse you make more problems for yourself from this. So ask questions about your problem to the right people. Now the real sensible question is how to identify the right people to tell your problems?

There are three types of people who can solve your problem.

1. First, who had the problem which you are suffering now and he has solved that problem, so you can ask him how he did it?
2. Second, who is currently going through the same problem which you have now, so you both can help each other to solve such problems. This is easier for you now in comparison to before because in that case, you are alone but now you have a company, which means less fear and more ideas about solving your problem.
3. Third, find a special person who has certified knowledge about your problem, who has experience in such a field. He has a fantastic record of solving such problems, so you can tell your problem to him without any hesitation because it is his profession regarding your problem.

Above such people you can freely tell your problem, without any fear, it is 100% sure you will be out of your problem without making fun of you. So it is necessary to identify the right people in your lives and for that process is above which you can try in any case of your life.

2. A sensible person does not want to make his true well-wishers unhappy with his misery.

It is not that a sad person, all his friends are ready to make fun of him. It is not that all the relatives of an unhappy person are there to make him more unhappy. It is not that when someone is sad, his neighbours will make his sorrow the medium of their gossip.

It may be that some friends or relatives or neighbours of a person are talking to him with a sincere heart only to know the condition of that unhappy person. There is nothing wrong in this that you are lightening your mind among your true loved ones. But a sensible person does not narrate the tales of his sorrow here thinking that I am going through my misery right now. But why should I hurt even these people with my sad words? I have met people who could solve my problems. After telling all my problems, I am on my way to solving them. And those who were going to make their means of making fun of my troubles and sorrows, I have already included them in the decision not to tell my problems through my filter system.

Now, these people are my true well-wishers. Neither of these people can solve my problems, but on the contrary, these people can also be unhappy with me. It is better that, I should forget my sorrow and become happy in their happiness. I should laugh a little. I should listen to jokes for a while. I should go out for a walk with them in the open sky. Why should I also recruit these people in the darkness of that misery? When I know that my sorrow is not going to last long, then why should I spoil them today with my today's misery.

"Let's be a little happy. Let's be a little wiser."

Part Four: Now our bike is about to go on a happy journey of relationships.

Running a relationship and riding a bike are the same thing. Maybe there will be people unhappy with relationships who will read this and say that it is very easy to ride a bike but it is very difficult to run a relationship. But I ask you, does your bike always run well? Perhaps you can say yes to this answer for now, but after thinking for some time you will come to know that even a bike gets damaged very often, which has to be dragged and taken to a mechanic.

So let's go to this new mechanic whose name is MIRROR OF OBSERVATION. But don't bring your bike, but bring the one you don't fix even if it is damaged. That is, your relationships, which you find very easy to connect, but very difficult to maintain and when there are disturbances like fear, anger, jealousy, doubt, quarrel, resentment in that relationship, then instead of resolving that relationship, You start running away from that relationship. If ever your bike got damaged in a crowded market, would you leave that bike there and run away? No, you will live with it, you will turn your eyes here and there, ask someone, is there a mechanic nearby? Who can fix my bike?

Then why do you leave a relationship and run away? It is not only necessary that you stay there, but it becomes your ultimate responsibility. No problem, now we will fulfil that responsibility better, that too by understanding many

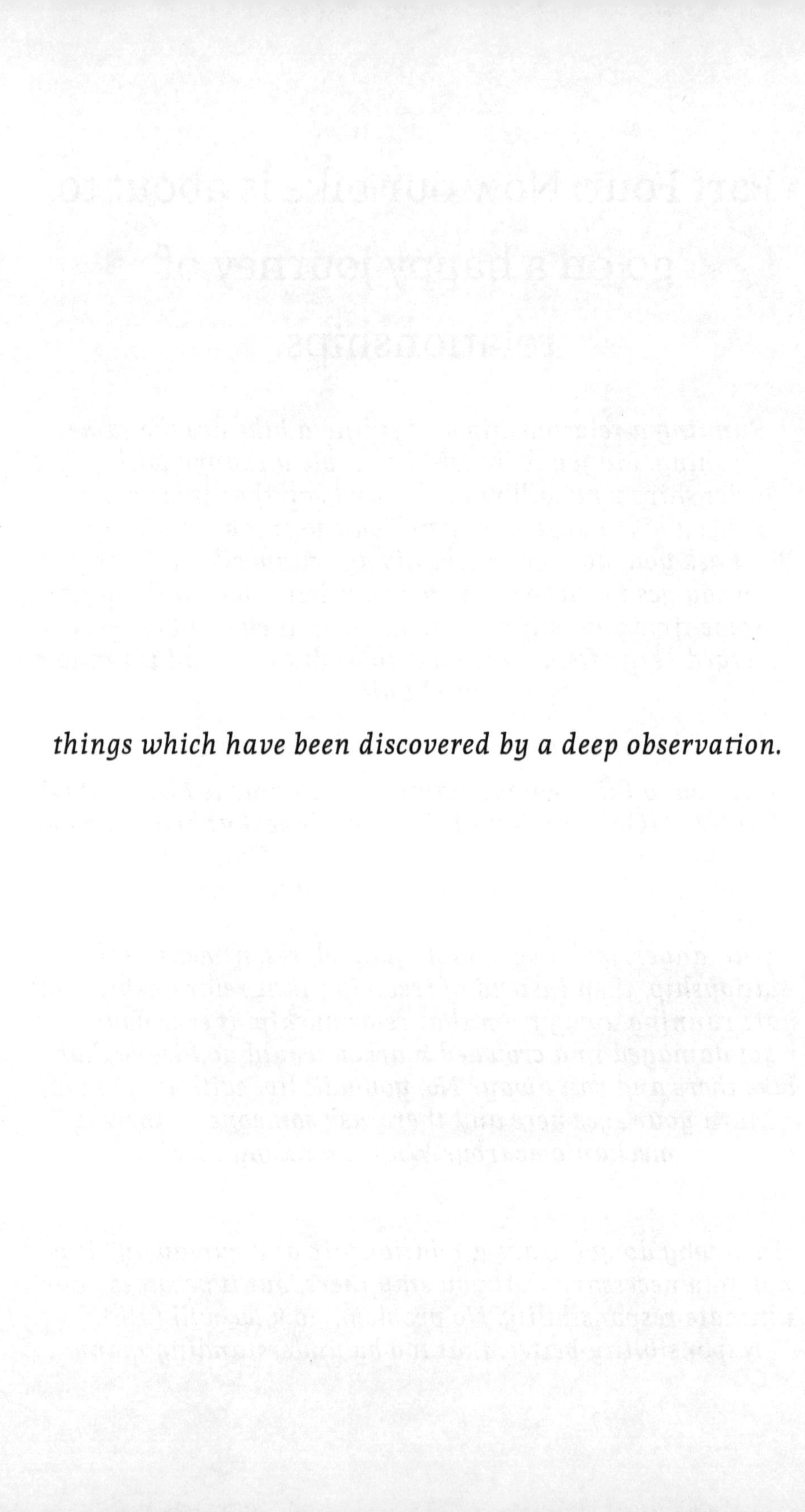

things which have been discovered by a deep observation.

THIRTEEN
INTRODUCTION

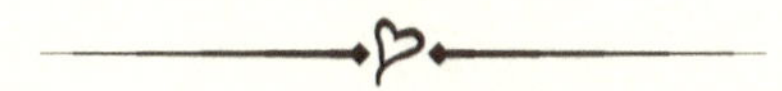

In any relationship, You always ask the same questions, how to handle this way?

- How can I make a good relationship between my wife and me?
- How to build a strong bond with my brother?
- How do I make a more beautiful relationship with my parents?

You seek answers to such questions every time in your life to improve any relationship. But can you see what is the commonality between them in all such questions? You use the sentence "how to do" the most in your questions while instead, you should look for the sentence "how to understand".

Let me explain all these math questions to you. First, you need to understand relationships and only then you can build a better relationship with someone. If you do not understand the arrangement of the relationship and how can you imagine that without knowing and understanding the relationship that you want to improve you will make it better. How? This is not possible at all.

For example, you want to operate a computer to make your office work easier but one thing is that you do not know the process of operating a computer; You do not know how to work on the computer. Now the question is, how can you do your work from a computer? Simple, first you need to learn computer from basic to advanced or learn computer at your convenience. After attending computer course classes, you will be ready to work on the computer.

Now look at this example by relating it to the relationship aspect, you will easily understand that first, you need to learn the process of relationship and the system of relationship. After that, you can manage your desires with any relationship.

FOURTEEN

HOW TO UNDERSTAND RELATIONSHIPS?

Now you one step forward, what is the process of understanding any relationship and it's the answer, observing that relationship which you want to make better and improving the bonding.

What is meant by observation of relation?

This means you need to pay attention to every aspect of your relationship. For example, one day you and your wife make your home a war room. You both shout at each other, both of them blame each other for the mistake that has caused a quarrel. Which one of you did but no one accepts the mistake. After all these quarrels you will be calm at some time. Both of you more and more you can fight for 1 hour, but after that, you will be angry and go to some room which may not be yours, then you will sit quietly in it. It is not that you will be fighting with each other all day. Maybe you are abusing your life partner even after going to that room, or maybe you are thinking of accepting your mistake. Any of these two things can happen, but the important thing is that,

After any quarrel, have you ever thought calmly about such questions, Like,

- What was the reason that the fight took place?
- Whose mistake was it in the true sense?
- If the mistake was mine, why didn't I accept my mistake?
- Why did I get into a fight?
- Would my ego get hurt if I accepted my mistake?
- Would it make me smaller than that person?
- If the mistake was of my life partner, then why was I cursing him instead of making him realize his mistake?
- The mistake that my life partner has made, will be cursing the life partner correct that mistake?
- If not, why am I spending my time doing other mistakes instead of correcting that mistake? Like this quarrel.

If you want to improve any of your relationships, If you want to save any relationship, then you have to adopt this analysis system. When you quarrel with someone you love, If you sleep with sadness on a sofa, then, except for the meaningless things, repeat all these questions in your mind and ask yourself the answer to all these. Which is called an understanding of a relationship.

If you get all these questions answered in that sad room, then next time you will not have any quarrel with that person either or that dispute will be settled in half an hour instead of 1 hour and if it will happen next time. The quarrel time will be 15 minutes.

Overall, you have to understand the relationship with whom, when and how to react.

- When do I have to calm down so that the quarrel does not proceed?
- How do I explain to that person that it is his fault, but I am not cursing him, but I am asking him to pay attention to the mistake that has been done?

It is not that understanding a relationship, You went on the Internet and read its definition and now you are hoping that my relationship will get better than before. It's not like this. Rather, understanding a relationship means that you have to understand the person with whom you have to improve your relationship.

FIFTEEN

WHAT IS ACTUAL LOVE?

I am talking about love, What is actual love and what do you understand love. According to my, there are two types of love.

First Unconditional love and Second Transactional love.

Now you must be thinking what kind of love is this? So I want to tell you that...

Transactional love.

That you think is love but it does not actually happen. It is clear from its name that love is transactional. Here I mean to say that when a person loves someone else, he also wants love in return. He will not love without getting love.

Let's understand from an EXAMPLE, There is a boy who loves a girl. They live together. The boy's expectations are fulfilled by what he wants from the girl and the girl's expectations are fulfilled by the boy.

- Both are happy because both are together.
- Both can do anything for each other as both are together.
- Both of them CARE each other, both also RESPECT each other as both are together.

Now come to **UNCONDITIONAL LOVE,**

Now, this example is the same as the EXAMPLE I mentioned above, if I remove the word "Together" in it? Then will it be called love or not? Will be called, because this is true love.

Now your next question will be that how? None of their expectations is being fulfilled, even then they love each other. Neither their PHYSICAL, MENTAL, EMOTIONAL are not fulfilling any desire, even then they love each other.

I mean to say that love is not a deal, nor any business in which the other party will give anything, only then you will pay its value. In which you like someone and that person will do something for you, only then you will do something for him or only then you will love him. Then how can you call it love? This is business, HIDDEN BUSINESS.

We need UNCONDITIONAL LOVE, not TRANSACTIONAL LOVE, whether we get nothing from that relationship, whether that person is with us or not, whatever it may be, from the beginning to the end, love is and will remain. UNCONDITIONAL LOVE applies not only to your life partner but also to your parents, your society, your country.

"I don't want anything, I just love you." If possible, you should also love me a little, otherwise, just let me see you for the rest of your life."

SIXTEEN

DON'T TAKE CHAPTER 15 IN THE WRONG WAY.

Everything has two sides, right and wrong. Good and bad. We need to do or not. The problem is not that there are two sides to something, but the real problem is which aspect is your tendency to lean more towards which you identify as right and wrong.

But the real game begins when you do some aspect of something more than what is needed to be done. It doesn't matter which side you have decided to go and after going there, you come to know that this part is called wrong by the world, therefore, I should not be here or this part is called good by the world That's why I have to follow this aspect more so that this world will give me the title of the best man because I follow the good things told by the world.

The problem is not when you follow the good aspect of anything, but the problem is that you don't even think for a second how good is that part if that thing is good?

- How far do I need to follow this aspect of the thing?
- What is its limit?
- Is it like the school exam that I need to score maximum marks from this exam so that I can top my class?
- Is this some kind of race that requires me to reach the finish line, can't win the shiny trophy without it?
- It is a good thing that you are aware that it is good to follow the right side of this thing and the left side of this thing that you should not see. But the question is, how good is good?

- And how bad to do could send us to jail?

These are the questions you need to ask yourself. Everyone knows what is good or what is bad. Everyone knows both sides of anything, which side of this thing is good and which side of this thing is bad. But not everyone knows that one thing of one side which we call good so,

How much do I need that good side?

How far do I have to go from what you call the bad side? The real question is that you have to find answers to these questions. How can I call you a wise man if you're looking for answers to a question you've already gotten? May I tell you that this person has common sense because you are talking about your common sense, If you have common sense then you can automatically call anything good or bad. But, how good is it for you to do this? How far should you get from the bad side of something? If you have found this answer or you are looking for answers to such questions then I can call you an intellectual who wants to improve his life.

The real goal.

After all these common-sense things, you need to find this chapter's real goal, which I want to tell you. I have written as per my title not to take Chapter 5 wrongly. what does this mean? Do I mean don't read that chapter, no, that's not what I meant. I have written important lines in chapter 5 that you need to go for unconditional love and transactional love is bad for your health and in unconditional love, you should not see love from the other side. You just have to do your duty. It doesn't matter if you love a person and that person decides that she will not give you even a piece of her share of love. Still, you have to go your own way and keep loving her whether the person accepts your love or not. You don't have to worry about that.

So this is the summary of Chapter 5 that I wrote about how you should play love. But my worry came out of my mind one day and asked me what if someone misunderstood what I have written in Chapter 5 about fulfilling love? What if someone starts using what I have written in the wrong way? Therefore,

I need to add another chapter to answer my concern.

When you saw a girl, you felt something different for her that had not happened to you when you saw another girl. You kept drowning in your thoughts and you wanted at that time that no one should save me from drowning. This kind of euphoria was taking over you. You were being happy for nothing. You can never stop yourself from seeing her. When people have trouble sleeping, they start worrying and they start shouting the name of a doctor. But when you were not sleeping at night, then you did not react like other people, or on the contrary, kept diving in her memories at night and without getting tired in the morning, even when your sleep was not complete, even then you had more agility than any common man. That too so that you can see that person once again. Your actions had changed. Your friends were looking at you with suspicion and were asking themselves in their mind, what has happened to him? Your friends came and woke you up and told you that your actions are like crazy. Seeing your friends' concern for you, again and again, you thought about your actions and what you thought you told your friends. Then you and your friends together conclude that you have fallen in love. You told your friends about that person and then decided that person will become your life partner.

Now from here, the real game starts.

Now you have come to know completely that I have fallen in love with that person and you have decided to tell your heart to that person. You took all kinds of advice from your friends that how you should keep your point in front of that person so that that person would agree to become your life partner. Decided one day, the weather was good. You have also put on good clothes and your future life partner is already good in your eyes. What do you want now?

You went to that person and you told her whatever was in your heart. That person didn't have the euphoria that you had at that time. That person simply denied you that she cannot be bound in your love. She apologized to you and left from there. For her, this story was over, maybe for you too this story would have ended here if my concern had not asked me that day,

If someone misuses Chapter 15?

So this story continues. You can't forget your girlfriend. That person's rejection of your love becomes a punishment for you. Still, you are not able to sleep at night but there is a lot of difference between earlier nights and now nights. Earlier you were not able to sleep because of their sweet sweet memories and now you are troubled by their separation.

You might not understand your girlfriend's answer, so you went to her again with the hope that she would agree this time. But then the same thing happened as before. She again refused you and she also insisted that now do not come to meet me.

Now you are sadder than before. The words of that person were making noise in your ears. You are not able to accept it that how did she say no to me. Now you became uncontrollable, you started chasing her, calling her again and again, You started going around her house, Wherever she went, you started following her. Now she is also completely troubled but not because she is in love with you but because she was tired of telling you that she doesn't love you even then you were not ready to accept it.

Why are you behaving like this with her?

If you truly love that person, then you do not bother her like this.

> "*We do any work wrong only when we do not have knowledge of that work or some greed is hidden behind doing that wrong thing and where there is greed, we do not love that work, but we love the fruit of that work.*"

If you truly loved that person, then your happiness would be in his happiness. If you like some work and that work is right even on a legal basis, even then how will you feel if someone stops you from doing that work? Then you will say that it is against my freedom. Perhaps because of this, you should also complain to that person in the police who is your right in the true sense.

So why don't you see these things in things like love? Why do you forget there that freedom is needed there too? There, everyone has their expectations. Everyone has their wishes. But why do you think only about your hopes, your desires? Why forget that that person also has a life. she also has different wishes. That person also wants to live life in her own way. Just like when someone stops you from doing the work of your choice, then you get upset, in the same way, if you stop her then she will also be upset.

Love is not imposed, love is made. Love is not just a word or a feeling, which has awakened within you and you have decided that the person I love should be with me now. No. It's not like that. If you are in love then good luck to you. You encountered the best aspect of life. If the person you love doesn't have the same feeling in her heart as you have, then you can't force that person in any way because you love that person and love will always bring happiness. Only you will be happy in the way you love, not the person you claim to love.

Respect is also a part of love.

Love is made up of so many things like the feelings that wake up in you, like the happiness that both the people should have in love and the respect which you forget that that too is an important part of love.

Respect does not mean praising a person because you are respecting him, when he comes to your house, welcome him well, take care of him. All this is the top layer of respect, which perhaps you often keep giving such false respect to people so that you get the benefit that you want from them.

Real respect is that in which the person you want to respect,

- You listen to her thoughts,
- Accept her views,
- Respect her wishes,
- Inspire that person to do the work which she enjoys.
- Not the work in which you are happy and you try to force that work on that person.

You should try to persuade the person whom you love, you should tell your heart to that person, there is nothing wrong in this, but wrong happens when that person has no intention of falling in love with you even then you force her. It is wrong.

After this, who will take care of your self-respect?

In all these things, you forget your self-respect and you take this self-respect lightly, while its effect on you is the most. Suppose you told your heart to the person whom you love but she refused to accept your love. You went to her again and again the person refused. You sat with friends, they came to know about it, they made fun of you, which you took to heart and it started getting bothered. Again you went to that person and then again you got disappointed and other people came to know that all this happened to you, those people started making fun of you.

Because of all these,

- You considered yourself to be less good than others,
- You started bringing all kinds of thoughts in your mind that I am hardly ugly, so she refused me,
- Maybe my financial situation is not good, so she refused me.
- Maybe I am low minded, so she refused me.

You started bringing such thoughts in your mind that you did not think before falling in love with that person. Now you are doubting your own potential with the abilities you were happy before falling in love with. Are you getting tired of those abilities now? This is something to think about.

The matter is simple, no one respects you or not, but you should respect yourself only then you will be able to move forward in your life. Not accepting your love from one person does not prove that you are not good. You ask your parents what is their opinion, do you think about your family, why they are loving you so much for so many years. If you didn't deserve that, why would they love you like that?

- Then, It's not about your being good or bad here.
- It's not about being beautiful or Unattractive here.
- It is not about you being rich or poor here.

It is only a matter of desires which is different for every person and which you should respect if you love in the right way and at the same time understand its meaning.

SEVENTEEN

ARE YOU HAPPY WITH ME?

So another question of your life or if you say so, only these questions which you often ask yourself like,

- Am I happy or not?
- Am I satisfied or not?
- How can I be happy?
- What work should I do so that I can get more joy in my life?

All these questions you ask yourself regularly in your life. Sometimes directly or indirectly but you ask such a question to yourself, not to any other person. Like,

- Have you ever asked your parents this question whether they are happy with you or not?
- Have you ever asked your life partner this question whether she feels pleasant with you or not?
- Do you ask such a question to your children whether they are satisfied with their school studies or not, or maybe they are interested in some other subject which they want to pursue, but because of your rude behaviour they are unable to live their life, They can't choose whatever they want?

Just once ask this question to your loved ones whether you are happy with me or not?

It is not just a question, but a tool to awaken a sense of importance in your loved one's mind for themselves. This is the kind of question in which you are giving authority to the person in front of you. In which she has got a special feel. By asking this question, you are telling that person how much she means to you. Especially in a married life, where there is a kind of dissatisfaction and in such a relationship, you need to pay special attention that your relationship does not get spoiled due to some reason.

Suppose you read this chapter and asked your life partner this question whether you are happy with me or not? That's all. Imagine that moment, what would be the reaction of your life partner at that time? There must be lines of questions drawn on his face. It is not that as soon as you ask your question, she will answer with a straight face,

- Yes, I am not happy with you.
- Or am I bored with this relationship?
- Or I don't want to be with you.

If your life partner is feeling such questions even in reality, even then she will not give you a direct answer. Because you have asked such a question that your life partner will not give a direct answer on it.

First of all, it is unique to ask such a question, because, before marriage, people pay a lot of attention to each other, but after marriage, there is a different kind of atmosphere, many responsibilities, respect for elders and in the face of this inflation, more and more working to earn money forces people to pay less attention to their life partner. That's why the importance of this question increases when you ask your life partner this question whether you are happy with me or not?

Your life partner will start caring about you instead of giving you a direct answer. On the contrary, your life partner will ask you what happened, is there any problem?

- Has something happened in the office?
- Has anyone said anything?
- Why are you talking about such strange things today?

Seeing so many cares, a different love will start awakening in you. But the purpose of this question is not yet known to you. Because like you ask this question to your life partner whether you are happy with me or not? Then love for you awakens in her heart. She starts looking at you with more respect than before and most importantly, she starts considering herself more important in your life than before.

Because it's not just a question. In this, you ask your life partner out of the bottle like a gin whether you are happy with me or not and your life partner considers herself as Allahdhin at that moment. Meaning that now all the wishes of her life are going to be fulfilled, she starts feeling like this.

Importance is a very big thing,

Which you cannot buy from any market. It happens inside you. It depends on you how much importance you give to others. Often you give importance in your life to those with whom you want to improve your relationship and from whom your life benefits.

- As you give a lot of importance to your boss so that he can increase your salary or promote you.
- Despite being the owner of a successful business, you give a lot of importance to the income tax officers so that they do not bother you unnecessarily.
- You give importance to your customers no matter how they treat you because you know that I am going to benefit from it.

But by giving fake importance to all these, you forget that you have to give importance even after going home. Your home truly contains the most important people in your life who are in dire need of your love and attention.

"*Because money gives peace for a moment, but despite having less money, you can live peacefully with good relationships.*"

If you go back to the question from which this chapter started, then that question is very important in your life. You should ask this question to your loved ones not one day, but every three-four days. Are you happy with me or not?

The first thing your loved ones will not give you is a direct answer and on the contrary, they will love you. she will start thinking about how much this person cares for me. You will get your morning tea without your asking. Your husband will bring a good gift for you in the evening after your question. Your wife will happily cook food for you.

Think about it, with just this one question, your few days have become very good. If you ask this question every few days, then the atmosphere of your house will be good for your whole life. Because people always need support whether they ask for it or not. They like it when someone cares for them and if that care is done by a loved one, then life starts enjoying it differently.

And secondly,

If your loved one has given a direct answer to your question, then in that condition, because of which your loved one is upset, try to solve it and after solving that problem, your relationship will be better than before.

You should think that if I do not ask such a question, then I would not have come to know about the suppressed problem which was in my life partner's mind since when and if I do not ask this question today, then it may be that my relationship gets worse. It is good that I came to know about the problem of my loved one or life partner in time from this question.

So go and ask her or him...

EIGHTEEN

WHAT ABOUT HER WISHES?

When you are going to start any work in your life. When you are going to take any action in your life. When you are going to implement any idea, any good thing in your life by which you believe that you can make your life better then you make up your mind to implement that idea. The point is not that you want a step forward in life, you want to start a work that benefits you, you want to follow an idea that can lead you in your life on the right path. This is good and life is all about progress. It does not matter how you progress, how you forward in your life.

- As you wish, whether you follow the right or wrong path in your life,
- You wish whether you believe in a good idea or not.
- It is your wish whether you want to start any work in your life or not.

The choice factor of your life is in your hands, if you have chosen the way of life according to your wish then you can call it a free life. The problem is not that you have chosen the things of your life according to your wish, but the real problem has arisen when you have chosen the things of someone else's life according to your wish. When you forget that freedom is not only for you but for the person whose life is going on according to your given conditions. If she fulfils your given conditions then she can live with you and if not then she has no right to live with you.

Let us understand all this with an example,

Let's say you want to start a business. You made a plan, you reassure your investors who are ready to be a part of your business, you have chosen an effective strategy for marketing your business product. Everything is right and ready for your dream setting.

All these your diligent efforts have earned you a serious response from your new customers who are interested in your business products. Now you are satisfied with your business plan and your investor has breathed in peace this time as there is no loss to their investment money rather they make a lot of profit from your business. Now you are eligible to pay more tax to the government of your country. So you are **happy with this business work in your life.**

If I may ask you what was your real objective of starting your business.

- Maybe you say, I want to earn more money.
- Maybe you say, I want to make my own identity out of this work,
- You may say, I don't want to disappoint my investors who put their money with their faith.
- Perhaps you want to introduce yourself as a successful man in this human society.

If you give me any one of the above answers to my question or all of these answers to my question then I will be satisfied with your answers but a little, not completely, that you are right. Because the answer I was looking for from your side is hidden within all these given answers because the real answer to my question is you want to be happy in your life, that's all.

Yes, this is the exact answer I was looking for. Because any of your work is his last stop or you can say his ultimate goal is happiness. You are always looking for happiness in your life, so you do many different types of work to satisfy your hunger for happiness. You can choose any work, its ultimate goal is happiness.

You work on your various needs like physical, mental, social, economic, emotional. You work for your various desires like I want to sing, I want to dance, I want to paint and many more things which you want to achieve in your life to fulfil the ultimate goal of your life, that is happiness.

It is not necessary that if you do or are going to do some work, then it will create wealth for you only then you will do that work and otherwise you will not do it even if you get real happiness from doing that work. you do what you want to do in your life if it is according to the law and there is nothing wrong with it. After all, You want to find happiness in your life.

But the real problem.

When you are thinking about your needs, your wants, your likes or dislikes. There is no problem with this. Because it's all about your happiness. Of course, you should be happy in life. But the real problem is when you don't consider these things, these natural rules to be important to someone else and then this real problem becomes even more catastrophic when you don't consider the aspect of happiness for your wife. You need to think about this serious matter which you always avoid by making excuses whenever such a topic comes to you.

Let's remember the story of your marriage.

- How a person who leaves her own house to make your home better.
- How your wife leaves all her sweet memories where she used to live.
- How your wife gives more importance to you than her parents after marriage.
- How does your wife leave her parents who raised her?
- Her brothers always protected her,
- Her sisters used to take the place of her friend group,
- All the members of her family always gave her lots of love and attention.
- She leaves all this for you because one day she becomes your wife.

After marriage, you got many things like,

- You have fulfilled various needs like physical, mental, emotional, social and sometimes financial from your partner.
- You got your dear children from her.

- Because of your wife you now have a lot of ideas on how to manage your home decor system.
- You have got a best friend for life from your wife whom you can talk to any time.

If I remind you of all the things that your wife has given you after marriage, I may have to write another book for your knowledge. But this chapter asks you the question what have you given to your wife after marriage?

In the initial stage of this chapter, I wrote about happiness that your ultimate goal of doing any work is happiness. If you do not get this ultimate goal then you will not be ready to do that activity in your life.

Am I allowed to do this?

One day a woman from another house becomes the wife of your house. So you should see this is also a kind of work and our law of life says that we do any work only to achieve the ultimate goal of our life which is happiness. So why do you think that the wife does not need the aspect of happiness? Or do you believe that the things that make you happy will also make your wife happy? Why do you think like this after marriage when your wife doesn't think even once about imposing her needs, her desires, her favourite work on you which gives her real happiness. Rather she does not do any work of her own desire which gives her true happiness. She always thinks that she should take permission from you to do the work of her wish. Why does she need to take permission from you to do anything and you act of your own will without anyone's permission. Why?

When she marries you she also has a lot of desires which she was thinking at the time of marriage and after marriage, those desires remain for a few days because in those few days she realizes what she wanted at that time and she was also thinking of working after marriage as per her wish, it was all in vain. She understands this.

- In your home, you start imposing your needs, your desires.
- You declare your intentions for your married life.
- You told her the vision of your life for the future.
- You said everything and still, you are saying what you want. But the thing is, who will think about her.

Like when you started a business. If I ask you why did you start the business? Maybe your answer will be like that I want to earn money for my family without this how will my family and I live my life. If you give me such an answer then I will agree but we should not forget that you not only have to survive in life but you also have to get happiness from your life.

Let's say you are not enjoying your work. This does not mean that you will close your business immediately. It will not happen but if you do not enjoy your work then you will look for some other work along with that work which gives you real happiness.

So my point is that you have taken different steps in life to satisfy your happiness so why don't you think the same for your wife who has taken a step of marriage.

- She also has desires,
- She also has needs.
- She also wants to live the life of her own free will as you live it.

Why does she have to take permission from you for her life decisions? You are married to a human being and not you have purchased a property which you claim I have a right over and I maintain this property as per my wish. If I want, I can build a lovely house on it or use it as a garbage can. You do not want to think so.

One day your wife comes to you and tells you that she also wants to do a job. You told her no saying that I earn enough for this house. You don't need to go out to earn money. It is not about making money every time.

- Maybe she wants to make her mark like you.
- Maybe she is not good at household chores and has a unique talent that she wants to show the world.
- Maybe she wants to fulfil the dream of her life that she was dreaming of since her birth and now she has the opportunity to fulfil it.

Anything is possible. It is enough that if she has one wish which is not wrong in any way, then she has every right to fulfil her wish. You have no right to stop her from doing her will in the name of care.

- Sometimes you stop her by saying that today's world is not safe for women.

- Sometimes you start having an unnecessary sense of insecurity.
- Sometimes you stop her from worrying about what society will say if my lady goes out for work.
- Sometimes you deter her by reminding her of her duties at home like babies need a mom. How can you expect to raise your children without a mother?

And many more things that you force to impose on her. You keep trying to make her feel that every problem in the world will start if she goes out of the house to do the things she wants without your permission.

That's why you keep trying all kinds of things to stop her, like begging her, showing her your anger, showing her your upset face and sometimes you use your physical force on her. You do all those dramas with her that can stop her from fulfilling her wish.

And she also calmly and lovingly accepts all your wishes just as your wishes are hers too. But despite this, she says no to you because she loves you. But you don't love her truly because love is about trust, love is about freedom, love is about your partner's desire which becomes your wish too. Like your wife who is always ready to follow your wish, which will make you happy her or not. Please think about your wife's happiness as nothing can handle any kind of pressure for a long time. One day it will prove to be a threat to you and your relationship.

NINETEEN

WHAT DO YOU EXPECT FROM YOUR BEST FRIENDS?

It is not just a simple question that I have asked you and you instead give me an answer which is not related to any part of our life where real actions and real thoughts are needed which helps us to understand our life better. Help us to live a better life. Or you are looking at this question as to the starting point for some philosophy talk and your mind is telling you right now that let's leave it. I know my friends and also know the relationship of my friendship with them. So I don't need to learn anything about friendship from this book.

You can think so. This is your mind and this is your life. Whatever way you want to drive the car of your life is your choice. But if you want to go on the right path in your life then you have to install the program of the learning system in your mind, so that you can learn from anything, from any place and can learn from any person's actions without disturbing your ego whatever is good for your life with which you can take fewer stumbling blocks in your life and soon learn from others.

Let us come back to our question which is the basis of this chapter. What do you expect from your best friends or should my question be,

What should you expect from your best friends?

I am sure you all must have come across this story from your lovely teachers and your weighty books while going to your school.

- That, you should make friends who will always stand by you in your difficult times.
- You should always look for those people in your life who are always working to solve your problems without your asking.
- If your friends do not know about the problems going on in your life and whenever you ask them for any kind of help, they give you a long list of excuses for not helping you. So you should not make such friends in your life and always look for that kind of friend in your life who will kill your enemy without you asking and happily eat prison food instead of you.

I am not going to mention in this chapter that this is all wrong knowledge which you got from your school life and you should not follow all these precious words from your teacher in your life. How can I forget those books from whose lines we tried to be a better person? All these things of our school days are true.

But my point is if you are looking for a true gold friend in your life,

- Who will never bother you with his/her duties?
- In your bad times, always appear in front of you like a god.
- Who is always ready to sacrifice his life for you even if you cheated on him with his girlfriend.

Then I am very sad for you because if you expect your friend to accept all these conditions then I am sure you must have seen every movie in your life in any cinema alone or with your parents but None of your friends was sitting next to you. Because you are living in an era where it is meaningless to expect a friend to follow such conditions. In this time, where you see any person doing any bad work, then you tell this one line to yourself and if someone is standing with you, then you tell that person, OH GOD, Kalyug has come, Kalyug has come. (Especially in India)

"According to Indian mythological books, Kalyuga means a time when bad deeds will be much greater than good deeds and can be easily done by human beings without any shame.

Adding to this it is also said that when there is an excess of bad deeds, then Lord Krishna will be born on earth in the form of Kalki and will destroy the unrighteous."

Where is the pure desi ghee?

In this Kalyuga time where everyone thinks about himself first and after that if he has time then he will think about others. We are living in such a time where goodness has become like a pure desi ghee (Indian melted butter) which is very difficult to get and if we get that kind of pure and unadulterated ghee then it becomes difficult for us to pay the expensive price for it.

You can see the same thing by adding it to the aspect of honesty. How difficult is an honest person's life in today's times as if he is still fighting for the freedom of this country? That honest person has to fight every moment, Every time he has to prove that he is right, He needs more time and more hard work in every government work than the common people because he is an honest person.

People think that the honest one does everything in the right way, so he does not need to pay any price for getting any work done like us. What do those people know who cook such delicious casserole with just a glance. Just be an honest person one day and see how he pays many times more than you.

Yes, you can say that an honest person does not pay the cost of money to get his work done. You are right then only he will be called honest who will follow the policy. But it is wrong to see only money as a price to pay.

Is there no value for that honest person's time which he has to spend many times more than the common people?

Like in a government office, an honest person waits for his turn by waiting in a line to get his work done. This is also a way to pay a price, just like you are not engaged in that line and have paid a huge amount for getting your work done before others. But here the value of that honest person's time is much more than the value of your money and especially the cost of his good thinking which no one can fix.

Is there no cost to the goodness of that honest person who, despite being right in every way, has to prove himself right again and again?

If you look closely at an honest person, you will find that the more honest a person is, the more upset he will be because he is doing such a thing which is very contrary to the work of today's world and when a person wants to swim in the opposite direction of the river. If he tries, he has to work harder and use more time than the common people.

By all these things I do not mean that you do not need to be honest. It is the same as if there is a bitter medicine which you always avoid eating but whenever you get sick then you have to eat that medicine right in your compulsion. In the same way, no matter how much you refuse good, if you want to live happily and peacefully in your life, then you have to adopt it.

After reading all this, it is obvious that there will be many questions in your mind that in a way this chapter is telling us about the increasing evils of Kalyuga and on the other hand it is talking about adopting the good things of life like a monk.

After all, what is the real purpose of this chapter?

And why the real purpose of the title of this chapter has not been revealed yet? If all these questions are roaming in your mind then I can call you a person who wants to live his life better.

The matter is simple, if you want to achieve all kinds of happiness and move forward as a better person during this Kalyuga, then you have to adopt all the good things of life as well as adopt the reality of today's life. Just like you cannot expect your friend to be endowed with all the qualities that you have taught from your school books and your loving teachers.

Yes, your friend should be a good person but it does not mean that he will always be ready to help you, so you have adopted him as your friend. None of your friends will always help you and it does not mean that your friends are not good. Everyone has some compulsion. Just as you want people to understand you, you also need to understand people.

Suppose you needed money at some point and you told your condition to your friend but your friend disappointed you at that time because he did not give you any kind of money related help. Due to this you got angry with your friend and started cursing him.

- But have you ever thought about why he refused you?
- Maybe he will have some compulsion,
- Maybe, his parents are not ready for this step,
- Maybe he doesn't have the money to help you.
- The reason can be anything, but without knowing that reason, you got angry with your friend.

And if you look at other aspects of friendship,

Then friendship is not only useful in times of sorrow. You have always heard such a line for friendship that friendship should always be that which always works in happiness and sorrow. But in your real life, you expect friendship with your friend only by catching this "sorrow" word and if that friend is not able to maintain his friendship in the moment of sorrow, then you get angry with him for life. Is it right to do so?

Have you ever thought that you have achieved some great success in your life and you have no one other than your family to celebrate that success because you have only looked at your friends from the sad side? Not from the aspect of happiness. What if you want to celebrate with people your same age? Despite being with your family, you will feel lonely in that happy moment because the importance of every human being and relationship is different. You cannot look at any relationship as equals.

Have you ever thought that if you ever want to go to any cinema to watch a movie, who will you go with? Can you always go to see every movie with your family? No, because every film's atmosphere is different and for every film, there are different types of people.

If you ever want to go on a trip, will you always go with family or go alone? Sometimes you have to say something that has been buried in your heart for a long time and which only your friend can reveal. Believe that you are very friendly with your parents, but this does not mean that you will only share everything with your parents.

Friendship is not the only thing you can expect in sorrow. Friendship has as much importance in happiness as it is in sorrow. I am not saying that you should be friends with bad people who are with you only on your good days, but I believe that you can never be completely satisfied with your friend. Because in today's time you will get both types of things in your friends. Good and evil too. It is up to you how you handle this thing.

"Friendship is very important iny our life, so don't consider it only as a companion of sorrow, but also look at it as a chance to party in happiness."

TWENTY

WHEN WILL MY PARENTS STOP YELLING AT ME?

All of you must have read many types of books in your life which claim to get rid of the troubles that have come or coming in life or you must have read the article of some such writers to amuse your hearts, whose opening words have subdued you or To make any work successful, the idea of acquiring knowledge and ideas related to it must have come to your mind.

In the same way, how do you handle very important, less important and only important relationships related to you in a good way? This type of thought must have also come to your mind at some point or the other or soon after reading the title of this chapter, this curiosity must have arisen in you that how should I handle my relationship with my parents properly?

Carrying the sack full of confusion of these relationships and "It's just my curiosity, I don't have a problem with the rest." Together with the help of such sentences, you all go out in such corridors where you meet different types of writers who write books only on subjects related to your curiosity and at the same time you are living in this modern era. Where there are two major and according to you the last resources available to solve any of your questions, that is YouTube and Google and in this corridor, you must have met the articles of bloggers like me or even better than me, who console you in a special way that, be patient. They give you suggestions to improve different types of relationships related to your life.

Often the claims or promises that are made are from the resources used to lighten your sack of curiosity mentioned above and when you come across these resources which they have in their own capacity and experience while fulfilling the objectives of your subjects, there can be right and wrong. But when their purpose does not serve to answer any of your questions correctly, then any thought and suggestion given to all these resources for any purpose are for you as if you asked for Gulab Jamun (is a milk-solid-based sweet popular in India) to eat and served Rasgulla (is a South Asian syrupy dessert popular in the Indian subcontinent) on your plate and you also taste that Rasgulla arguing to yourself that what difference does it make, it is also a good sweet.

In this way, your work can go on in enjoying sweets. There you can deal with situations like this, but when it comes to questions full of intense curiosity, which are directly related to your life and what about the relationships of those people in that life too, who are very strongly connected to you. Without whom you cannot even imagine your life.

So such questions which are related to the important relationships of your life, then it is very important for you to keep in mind that what question you have come out in search of and what answer you are getting in return. Is that answer proving to be completely correct for my question or is my question itself wrong. In this way, it is very important to analyze yourself and the questions asked by you for important issues related to your relationships.

What I mean by analysis is that you give birth to such a question in your mind that,

How should I improve my relationship with my parents? Whereas your question should have been, How did I understand the relationship related to my parents? How do understand the important relationships related to life? Your curiosity sack should be like this whenever you come across books written on the dimensions of relationships or today's wells who quench your thirst for questions in a jiffy, YouTube and Google.

When you do not understand a question, how can you go to find its solution? It is more important to understand relationships than to handle them, then only you will be able to handle them well and make them better.

Keeping this in mind, now we come to our today's title, about which you have been wanting to read since when and why not, because of this title, you have been able to travel this far.

Look carefully, I mentioned the word "Yelling" in the title of this chapter. If I wanted, I could have chosen a simple type of title for this chapter as well. Was it my intention to attract you, which is why I chose this different caste title used by very few writers of this type? No, this time my intention is more than your invaluable attraction, I found it necessary to make you pay attention to those things or actions that happen to you in the right way, prick you, bother you.

> **"We never have trouble with relationships in our human life, so we use our intellectual and practical abilities to create many relationships according to our own taste. Whose number is much more than the relationships made by all kinds of living beings in this world. The real problem comes from the behaviour those relationships do for us.**
> **"**

After reading this wonderful thought, you must have considered the animal species to be more intelligent than yourself based on this matter for some time only. Yes, your opinion may be right and there is a real reason for that. That reason is called "option". Animals do not have the option of making different kinds of relationships or they do not want to make choices in their life like the more human race.

If you take a look at the system of building relationships of mankind, then you will come to know that relationships in your life are made based on different needs, compulsions and especially your emotional attitude which is sometimes implemented based on mental power but the non-human species is ignorant of words like a necessity, compulsion and emotion, so what will they follow while making their relationships?

Overall, if you add the math of the conclusion, it is coming out that the human race works to make more and more relationships and the non-human race works to handle the relationships that it has.

When you have come to know that you have a lot of relationships and when you become unhappy with some of those relationships, then at that time the thought of donating to someone also comes to your mind.

With the abundance of relationships, you also have different ways of dealing with them, the ways which you want or not, you have to use them in your everyday life. In the same way, the way of maintaining the relationship related to parents is also hidden, but by unveiling it now, you will not get any benefit unless you understand that relationship itself.

You are more interested in the upper layers of this relationship rather than understanding it.

- Why do my parents shout at me about everything?
- Why do they keep giving directions like the traffic police at every stage of life?
- Didn't they know? Now my age has touched that line which is known in this world as maturity.

And to understand this, you have to know the reasons based on which the behaviour of your parents and together with my chapter stands.

Now it's time to test the foundation. For a long time, we were happy to see only the top structure of the house. I mean it's time to find out the reasons why you have hurt your cognitive abilities so far.

The primary reason:

The situation of your beloved parent, where every conversation made with you has displeasure, resentment, making you realize your mistake and the absence of special actions like harshness in their voice, tells that your parents consider you an intelligent son. Your parents have given you the status of a child worthy of their trust in their minds during this time of sinners.

Now, what else do you need from your life when your birth creator has accepted you as a wise person. Maybe your time is not supporting you right now? You are not able to do the kind of work that your parents expect you to do. You have to cross many more difficult stages than others to become or achieve something in life. Or it may also be that due to you some trouble has entered the house and even then the behaviour of your parents is the same as it remains in normal days.

If you are in such a situation and especially your parents are not losing their temper, then you can understand that they are following this first reason very well. Your parents' behaviour like this is not caused by twirling a magic wand. One day your parents were scolding you for some reason and you chanted a magic mantra and now you unintentionally break the most expensive bouquet in your house, your parents still look at you as If you have secured the first position in your class.

Your parents' good behaviour towards you, that too in your bad times full of mistakes, simply means that you will be such a person in your past who thinks of following the thoughts of Lord Rama every day. The meaning of this is that you must have obeyed everything your parents say. You must be always involved in such activities at your school level, due to which your smiling picture will be visible to your parents every year on the front page of the newspaper coming to your home. You must have done everything in your life in such a way that the people around you would have accepted the creator of that work. Overall, your image will be good in the eyes of your parents, due to which there will be no difference in the behaviour of your parents towards you due to any kind of mistake from you in recent times. (Wrong behaviour with women will not be included in this mistake)

The Secondary Reason:

You follow exactly the opposite of what was mentioned in the first reason. Your parents have established such status for you in their mind, which no child would expect from their parents. The meaning of these words is that your parents look at you, not like Ram, not even like Ravana, but as such a foolish person whose every decision is not his own. Your parents have accepted that our children are innocent who not only know the world but do not even try to know that world.

If someone's parents are looking at him from this point of view, even then you should assume that they would have been generally calm in his dealings with his children and those who were looking for answers by reading the title of this chapter "When will my parents stop yelling at me? So in response to those people, I would like to present this type of situation, in which any parent shouts at his child or says in the right way, then after a time, they stop wasting time in showing the path of life.

Now based on these two reasons, you have to organize wrestling in your mind with the question of the title of this chapter, so that you can determine in which situation you are present, due to which your dear parents have stopped shouting at you.

If you conclude from this analysis that you do not find yourself in any of the two reasons mentioned in this chapter and at the same time your parents continue to get their birthrights through you, that is, your Parents scold you, yell at you and treat you like a small child on everything, So you should thank your parents right now because your parents neither consider you intelligent and obedient nor do you include you in the status of a foolish person.

With this, you must have got the answer to the question of your mind as well as the answer to this title.

TWENTY-ONE
HOW SHOULD WE TREAT GUESTS?

It is determined based on the behaviour of a guest who came to the house and where the situation of the decision arises, it simply means that by choosing one of the more than one option available while doing a task, to take that work to its real destination.

Perhaps right now your body is getting signals of some disturbance in your brain structures because before today you and your brain may have followed the same age-old system of dealing with guests at home and just like your brain, When he came to know about the new method of dealing with a guest who came home, then your mind fell into the state of rebellion and you started scratching your head with the help of the lovely fingers of your hands to stop that rebellion.

But you also know that just scratching the head does not stop any rebellion, because the meaning of rebellion is that the decision of a person or a particular group of people related to the important aspect of their life is done by an official person or the prominent people of that group and when the decision taken for that person or that group of people makes them realize the possibility of any harm in their life, then that person or that particular group decides to revolt against the decision taken.

This means that until they do not understand the decision taken for the important aspect related to their life. Until that person or that particular group comes to know that the decision taken for them will fully contribute to the progress in their life and which will only benefit them instead of any kind of loss, then they The person or Those people will continue to oppose everything related to the decision.

Even with the thoughts of this chapter, till your mind does not conclude that these new types of ideas which are directly related to the behaviour of guests are beneficial in the true sense or not or just empty talk. To solve these confusions in your mind, you try to know the circumstances due to which challenges the treatment of guests that have been going on for centuries.

One of these confusions in your mind will also be that you always have to behave in the same way with guests and in that way, a guest who came to your house always leaves happily, Moreover, he also appreciates your hospitality among your other relatives. Then what do you need for a new way where a guest who came to your house in the same way as before and both of you are satisfied.

I want to give a ray of happiness to your satisfaction by saying that the age-old behaviour used by you is completely effective in the behaviour of a type of guest coming home.

How we should treat a guest coming home?

It depends on the situation created by them. The first situation is where you do not need to learn or adopt anything new.

- If a guest who comes to your house starts his talk with "goodness" and you keep feeling that good till the end of the conversation established by him,
- If the words spoken by your guest do not include a bad feeling for another person or group or for the activities they have done,
- If a guest who comes to your house gives you a good lesson or does not give a good lesson, then he does not go to teach you any bad thing, then you know how to deal with the guests, there is no need for you to acquire any kind of knowledge about it.

But for those who have forgotten the way of hospitality or those who feel a little dissatisfied in the use of their methods, take a look around.

Whenever a guest is about to place his holy feet at your house, there are two types of position details hidden behind him,

One is the symbolic position,

In which the guest before entering your house gives you the information of his arrival.

Second, the unintentional movement situation,

In which the guest truly follows his rights. This means that your guest uninvited and without notice, any day, any time, for any reason, comes and sits on the comfortable sofa of your home. Now that your guest uses the most used item by your family in your house, that is, he has been seated on the sofa of your house, then his hospitality will not be just by staring. For hospitality, first of all, you have to give them a grand welcome,

- "You don't even come",
- "After how much time have you got leisure",
- "Today I am very happy that you have chosen the way to come to my house",

In this way, you have to choose the sentences that make the guest feel familiar. After this, you will request them to sit and will try to know about the journey which your guest has travelled. You will give him a glass of water, and for as long as your guest stays at your house, you will have made him drink as much water as he hasn't in his entire life.

> "*The time has come to find the most expensive and long-hidden utensils of the house because a guest has arrived at your house.*"

Now the guest will be taken care of with a loving atmosphere and in this hospitality, you will do good to the guest's growing stomach, Breakfast with sweet tea in the morning, lunch full of dishes from all over the world and more than food at night, you and your guests get drenched in the rain of nostalgia and when the guest is so much filled with your hospitality that now he wants to go home but you too will keep trying unsuccessfully to stop him with your sweet words.

Now we will know about the second situation,

Due to this, today I am using the ink of my lovely pen to write guest texts. In this situation, instead of giving any details from my side, I would request you to go in the opposite direction of the sentences used in the first situation. That is if a guest arrives at your house, He takes part in the activities exactly opposite to the activities present in the first situation. Like,

- If a guest who comes to your house starts his talk with "evil" and you keep feeling that evil feeling till the end of the conversation established by him,
- If the words spoken by your guest include a bad sense of belonging to another person or group or activities undertaken by them,
- If a guest who came to your house tries to teach you some bad thing instead of giving you a good lesson, then what form you have to give to your hospitality, that is the ultimate point of this chapter.

To fulfil the purpose of this new hospitality, you have to adapt to the two circumstances. What I mean by the circumstances is that in which season your guest has entered your house, your further strategy will be decided accordingly.

Hot Summer

If your guest has come to visit you in the hot summer season and he has completely moulded his conversation in the second situation I thought, then,

- First of all, fan or AC any such facility which even though it is summer season Its just opposite effect makes your guest feel.
- You should immediately stop the mediums providing all those facilities which force them to sit at your house.
- You should avoid giving them all the food and drinks that will help them to stay at your home. Like cold water. That cold drink whose advertisement comes again and again on every channel of your home TV. That glass of juice full of ice cream that your guest has wanted to drink.

Now let's enjoy a little cold.

Meaning that in the winter season, how do you have to deal with the guest who came to your house. I know that my reader is one of the most intelligent readers of this world, so he must have understood in a moment how he has to deal with the guest who came home in this season. During the winter season,

- As you ask the wings of your house to rest, in the same way, when a guest comes, you should not give any such order. Meaning that you have to keep that fan of your house at its full capacity where you and your guest are sitting.
- Far from using the air conditioner in the winter season, you avoid even taking its name, but you have to take the name of the AC because of the guest coming home and take it to your coldest place.
- You have to make the atmosphere of your house such that the guest who comes home should like to stay outside the house rather than staying at your house.

All this talk is for laughs, Perhaps you will be at the peak of your laughter right now after all these humour related things. Of course, you can laugh and you can take all these things like sarcasm, but you must know the real reason for doing the activities mentioned in all these things and at the same time you should also take this wonderful idea to your attention.

> **""If your neighbour throws garbage at your house, you will report it to the police, but you do not report the neighbour who always throws garbage on your scalp, but one day if that neighbour forgets to throw garbage on you, then you feel that the day Going blank.**
> **: Unknown "**
> **"**

Here, if you try to find out the meaning of the word garbage used in this thought, then you will find that your neighbour daily tells you that type of news which mostly includes the flaws and evils of the people and the activities done by them.

Many of you must be thinking that this book is taking us on the wrong path. Did I choose this book to adopt this wrong path, which in a way is emphasizing treating guests who come home in the wrong way? It is justified to worry about you in this way and our Hindu religion also, the guests have been given the status of God, but you think a little that God speaks badly? Sharing bad thoughts? About any subject matter? About the activities undertaken by any individual or group. Then how did such a guest become God? It's something to think about.

You are giving him **GREEN SIGNALS**

Think about the way I have described the things to be done in the second situation. Think carefully about your hospitality, which you inflict on a guest who has come to your house.

"As a guest came, and as soon as he arrived, he started speaking bad, about anyone, You did not say anything, on the contrary, you asked your dear guest to sit. Right now he is doing evil. You have now started giving tea, giving water, etc, etc, taking care of him. He is still saying bad words. You thought carefully that you are giving him "GREEN SIGNALS". You are not stopping him, but by taking care, you are encouraging your guest to speak more badly.

"Look at the thought, "we become human by our thinking, otherwise what is the difference between animal and human""

TWENTY-TWO
LIVE-IN RELATIONSHIP

In today's era, people like to dream of this relationship, especially those young couples who want to understand once before getting into the social and legal bond of marriage, that yearning, to meet each other. The yearning of making eye-to-eye contact with each other, holding each other's hand and measuring the heartbeat, will it remain in our midst even after marriage?

Overall, a future married couple wants to know the behaviour of my lover before marriage, will he remain the same after marriage or Will I find a new incarnation in him to some extent or wholly in the form of my husband or wife? And if my life partner behaves against my expectations, will I be able to live with that behaviour for the rest of my life?

It becomes your responsibility and responsibility of this chapter to know the full meaning of the relationship you are planning to jump into, then only we will be able to find the legal questions related to it.

Live-in Relationship -

"When two people (especially of the opposite sex) live under the same roof and have a relationship with each other, including physical relations, with each other's consent. But there is a drawback in this and it should be there too, without it it will not be called a live-in-relationship but a marriage. Yes, even if they are not married, participating in all those activities that husband and wife do together after marriage, then this unique relationship will be called a live-in relationship.

Now let's come to those legal rights,

So that you can escape from that nightmare in which you and your beloved partner are in a nice hotel room. Where you were about to fulfil your old wish through your partner, the police force enters the room like an unwanted, uninvited guest and a criminal's stick is about to hit your butt, and your nightmare is broken. You wake up from sleep that too without exercising with drops of sweat.

Do you want this dream of yours to come true? Obviously, your answer will be no and if ever any activity related to this dream happens to you, then what legal rights exist with you so that you can save your terrible dream from coming true.

First of all, those questions have to be laid on which a beautiful palace of legal rights related to live-in relationships can be built.

1. Is live-in-relationship valid in India or is such a web of confusion being woven around us through western culture films, so that we can stand against the laws of our country?
2. We have started living like husband and wife without taking the holy rounds of marriage, so will our honeymoon moments now pass in lock-up?
3. Some of my neighbours where I live are jealous of my live-in-relationship. So can they take any legal action against me?
4. Tell me as soon as possible all those legal rights related to live-in relationships, so that I can shut the mouth of this stupid talking society.
5. Together I also want to know that who is entitled to keep these rights?

The foundation is ready, the goods have arrived, you who are responsible have made a great map of the palace. Now my work because here I am also a labourer and I am also an artisan who will effectively carve out the answers to your questions.

Vishwa Guru to Guru.

India was in the position of a Vishwa Guru since ancient times. Such a Guru from whom different types of people used to come from different countries to get knowledge. Now the situation has changed or the way of thinking of the people has changed, but now there is no Vishwa Guru but the position of Guru has been taken by these western countries, that too in this modern era where we get any kind of education from anyone. It is not necessary to go to them to do it. Now the medium of transaction of education is the TV channels associated with the cultures of the world, the films and programs they show, which indirectly promise that we will promote the most forward and open thinking of this modern era.

If not all of us are suffering from Alzheimer's disease then how can we forget all those social media applications which were specially invented to connect with distant friends and relatives.

> *"But there is a saying that good habits and bad addictions are associated with every work from the very beginning. It completely depends on you who, your eyes fall first and on whom you stay till the end. All of us have also been engaged in realizing this proverb with our bad addictions to narrate this proverb to our descendants. Many of us may have emerged as the most liked friend or relative on social media, but in real life, which is not about charging but breathing, we will be the least host of people.*
> *"*

All these resources only after using which you get recognition as a person of modern times. Above all and in all this, what we see, what we hear and with full dedication, we all believe that now we have to indulge in such activities because "the trend is going on these days" repeating this sentence. We console ourselves to do that work which we have seen on TV, social media and OTT forums in recent times.

Now if we tease the wires of the country of India,

Then we will find that the sparks of live-in relationships have become common here. Especially for the metropolitan cities of our country, where a large number of people live under one roof without being bound by any social and legal bond and together pay the electricity bills of that house and their wishes through each other.

- After using so many words that lengthen this chapter, I want to give you the happy news that there is no law on live-in relation to our country. Nor has any MP thought of discussing it in Parliament to make an Act.

If India is a matter of country and population is not mentioned, how can it be done? It may be that while writing this chapter of mine, the children of many mothers of this country must have started kicking to come out of the womb.

If there is such a large population in a country and there is no sound of falling utensils, can it happen?

That is, as many people as many problems and many problems in them become so serious that they have to resort to law to overcome them. That is, many lawsuits and in those cases too many cases related to human-chosen relationships i.e. marriages and many cases come from those future life partners, taking inspiration from whom the words of live-in-relationship are being threaded in this chapter. Because the courts, having no law relating to this subject, came to them the cases from all over the world, which directly and indirectly form the basis of live-in-relationship, so the decisions on those cases by the courts of different grades from time to time are called seen as a law.

For this reason, the conclusions drawn by the various courts that have been heard so far in various kinds of relationship cases are that without marriage and without giving the huge amount of the rituals of "Muh-Dhikhai" to your sisters-in-law, You can spend the first night of your unmarried life comfortably with your future life partner. That is, you can live in a live-in relationship. The Constitution of India has given you those fundamental rights, because of which you can feel freedom and do anything with anyone, staying within the ambit of the law.

Another excuse that leads to a live-in relationship.

But, before realizing this wonderful freedom, you need to remember that ever you have voted your beloved future leader of any position with pride in any election in this country, that is, are you 18 years old? When you answer yes to this question or laugh after reading this, then you are made for a live-in relationship.

Have you ever had such a wonderful accident that you have gone to the market to buy an essential item and you have found not one but two or three items with the purchased item without paying for that items? Don't be sad if you haven't gone through such beautiful moments. This dream shown by me is going to be fulfilled through this live-in relationship, because the benefit is being given to the live-in relationship.

Just like to get married, it is necessary to cross the age fixed by law. Like if a male person has not turned 21 years old or his partner is female, then if she has not turned 18, the fight of his girlfriend and boyfriend will not change in the fights of the husband and wife. That means they will not be able to get married legally.

But here it is a matter of profit, so for that, the people of the male caste will not need to feed a fish for 21 years. They will be able to lift the feeling of being married without being married only after they turn 18 by living in a live-in relationship with their partner.

A Love Story

It is the duty of all of us as conscious citizens that such great judges are present in our judiciary whose open and shoulder-to-shoulder thinking with today's society has allowed live-in-relationship on legal lines. If we do not run after the names and fulfil our purpose directly, that means fulfilling our selfishness for a while and understanding the real meaning in the story, then the time in our life and life will thank us.

The boy in the story was 18 years old and the girl was 21 years old. You see, what a coincidence that along with their thinking, their age is also the exact opposite of the age prescribed by law. What can we do now, a great person has said that love is neither by age, nor caste, nor colour, nor wealth nor poverty. It is just as if a pleasant wind blows, the intoxication of love falls.

These two love couples also fell in love without seeing each other's birth certificate and they got married after going there, miles away from home where no one comes and goes, except the priest who recites the mantra.

In a male-dominated society, where the mistake committed by the boy is seen only by connecting it with the enthusiasm of his youth, what will the father of that boy do? But in this society, when a girl takes steps that have not been taken yet outside the house, then the blood pressure of the girl's father increases and he starts trying to find the girl.

The end of this love story was also the same as always happens with a lovely love story, that is pain. But in this story, the girl's father went a step ahead, he appealed to the court and the result was that the court declared this new marriage invalid, becoming support in the pain of a father, his lost daughter who got separated of her own free will. had reunited her with his father. But the boy also turned out to be Majnu, he too knocked on the door of the Supreme Court without giving up.

> "Honourable Mr Justice A.K. Sikri Honorable Mr Justice Ashok Bhushan, while giving his views on this, said that the marriage should not have been declared invalid and even if declared, it is not a crime to live together after crossing the age prescribed by the Constitution."

Now the story of an unhappy judge who hears the divorce cases.

In this whole world, anyone who can show courage and interest in resolving the mutual dispute between a husband and wife is a judge of a Family Court. Many issues related to marriage come to them and many relationships come on the verge of breaking up and filing a divorce application in court.

- Suppose I have borrowed some rupees from you and the number of those rupees is such that you are not able to sleep peacefully at night. Now two types of my fantasies are connected in this supposed story. On one hand, I have given you back the money that you had lent to me in time. Second, it has been two years since you asked for the money given to me on the loan, but I am shamelessly telling you every day with new types of excuses.

I ask you if you ever want to lend money to someone, which one of these imaginations would you like to bring into reality? The first one.

Similar is the case in divorce matters, where a partner hates his life partner so much that he wants to separate from her legally with his heart. But the same other partner has filled so much love in her heart that forgetting all the quarrels with her life partner, she still wants to be together. It means that she does not want to divorce her partner.

In such matters, two people are the most unhappy and two people are the happiest.

Among the unhappy people,

One is the life partner who loves her beloved partner so much that by ignoring all the mistakes committed by him (including filing for divorce) neither with her mind nor with legally she wants to separate from her partner.

The second unhappy person is the one who is not personally interested in this issue, yet because of being associated with the judiciary of a country and because of his hard-earned government job as a judge, he has to solve this divorce issue. He has to use his mental capacity and precious time with a sad heart.

Now it's the turn of smiling faces who are very happy with this divorce issue.

1. The first person is the one who wants to be separated from his life partner under any circumstances. He wants to get divorced by forgetting all the expensive expenses made in his marriage and all the beautiful moments he spent with his life partner.
2. Second, that happy person, who in any case wants that this issue should continue in the court for a long time so that he can enjoy life to the fullest through his advocacy profession.

If you ask a married person what is your worst dream, then he will say straight away that whenever I want to get divorced, my life partner should give me divorce like a birthday gift. I don't have to go round any courts and fill the pockets of lawyers for 8-10 years.

It is not that you will become "Aladdin" after getting married and on asking anything from your partner, he will accept all your wishes without thinking like "Jin". Keeping this in mind, some sensible and helpless person invented this great, non-marriage relationship that participates in activities like marriage. So that in future any loving couple does not have to go through difficult times like divorce to separate from each other.

While discussing the issue of live-in relation, how can we forget that society which is always against the thinking that boycotts every old custom?

On the one hand, a society that lives with much orthodox thinking. Their rules, their customs always benefit only one class. Whether you choose that class from richness and poverty, whether you choose that class from the increasing sex ratio of male-female or choose from the age-old high caste pride and low caste untouchability. Always the rules made by the same section of society for their benefit or "our ancestors did the same" in this way, showing their obedient quality, everyone tries to pass on the already existing tradition to their descendants, therefore, a Society maintains its orthodox thinking.

If we all are aware of this face of society, then we must also know that a relationship like a live-in-relationship is considered nothing but a bad thought in the streets of India.

But the question comes out here who will boycott the live-in relationship? Who would stand up against this wonderful relationship the most?

- People who know you, with whom you live. Whether they are the people of the house, whether the people of your locality and even those people of your city who recognize you as a friend and relative. Between them and only because of their taunts, you will not be able to live the beautiful relationship of your live-in relationship.

But you have established this relationship in such a house, in such a locality and in such a city where the number of people who know you is very less and even those who know you, their thinking welcomes this relationship openly, then at that place and In that environment, you can live with that unique relationship of yours. Because society mostly boycotts those whom they know well.

Do you know or have forgotten section 497?

When we have realized from all these discourses that a tradition or rule followed by any society is not beneficial for every section of the society. Some class is angry with the injustice done to them by society, but instead of revolting, that class comes home understanding the blessings of God.

Keeping this important point in mind, those people of the society who do not give themselves the status of any special class, indicate their understanding and generosity. Such people make laws for every section of the society, for equality in every field. Such a law can stand against injustice by looking at everyone equally and can become the voice of those who need justice in the true sense.

These are all the good things that we the people of a nation expect from the constitution of our nation and the system of justice that it runs.

- But what if a law only makes one section of society feel inequality?
- Whose laws should always satisfy only one section of the society?
- And due to which the deprived class concluded that what was the difference between this law and the thinking of the orthodox society?

The Law of India's legal system stood in the dock of such questions. But as I have told above through my words some sensible and kind people come out of every inequality like a lamp of light and prove by their deeds that we do not belong to any particular class, we All are one.

A five-judge Supreme Court bench declared adultery unconstitutional in September 2018.

Perhaps after reading this, something is going on in the wires of your mind that after all what is this law and why is it suddenly being mentioned in live-in relationships? If these kinds of questions are being asked by your mind then there is no need to drink hard tea to wake yourself up. Because of your curiosity, you did not even sleep till this stage of this chapter. That's a good thing for me and your brain's treasure trove of good lessons.

So the answer to the questions is that, when a man and a woman have not taken seven rounds of marriage according to the rituals, taking a burning fire as a witness and amid a large crowd of people, in an expensive program of marriage, yet Considering that man as her husband or even better, she has participated in the activities done on the honeymoon with him and after this beautiful night, if the real husband of that woman and the family members of that husband comes to know about this tragic incident, then it is called Adultery and when the real husband of that woman instead of turning his anger into a scuffle, he takes recourse to the law with understanding. In which that husband, based on Section 497 Indian Penal Code, tries to get the lover of that wife to be punished by the court with imprisonment of 5 years and fine or it would be correct to say that he used to. Because our Supreme Court has declared this law unconstitutional saying that it does not give a feeling of equality to the women society.

Now many of you must be thinking that where has the sense of equality and inequality come from here? On the contrary, the law has given the woman the option of another husband. This law gives a signal to the woman and her lover that now we are legally free.

> *"No, it is your freedom to interpret something in your own way, but to apply the meaning of the same thing in reality and people are harmed by that meaning, whether the loss is physical, mental, emotional, financial or social, You don't have the freedom to do that harm."*

Here too, you have misinterpreted these questions and whose loss may probably be to your close ones. To avoid this loss, we should also know the other aspect of this law so that the meaning taken by us is not harmful.

The unconstitutional law in which it was being mentioned that a husband can take revenge for the injustice done to him by the wife's lover with the help of law, but the same law did not give any legal rights to a woman like a man when she came in such a situation. Meaning that a man could ensnare his unfaithful wife's lover in a legal trap, but a woman could not inflict any legal anger on her husband's girlfriend. Due to this inequality, this law was thrown out of the book of law itself. But the husband or wife can avenge their infidelity by filing a divorce application in court and it becomes easier for a court to divorce a married couple on this ground.

Our second question was,

What is the meaning of this legal thing with a live-in relationship? So if a man and a woman keep a relationship with each other without marriage, which includes physical, then that is called a live-in relationship. What difference does it make whether one or both of the women or men have already been married to someone else? Now no law used to give a separate identity to this relationship, so now it is recognized in the law and for new cases that have come in a family court, this adultery is known as a live-in relationship.

Now in this part, I am going to tell you the story of the misconceptions of those people who see live-in relationships only from the beginning of a new marriage. They do not even dream of a life full of other responsibilities.

Have you ever seen people of any country, society fighting for their duties for any issue? Yes, a large number of people have certainly expressed their indignation to remind any institution, government or executive system of its duty. Like how the heart of the people goes when the price of petrol increases. They get angry to such an extent that they also affect the rest of the good works of the government due to the anger of the rising petrol. Every step taken by the government for the welfare of the people is looked upon with suspicion. You must have seen it very rare that the same people made any effort on their behalf to stop the increasing pollution from traffic or like a strike at the time of infringement of their rights.

In the same way, before going into a live-in relationship, you need to understand that your physical, mental, emotional and financial rights will not only be fulfilled in that relationship, but if not by your will, then you will have to legally take your responsibilities towards that relationship. You will also have to participate in completing it.

As in a live-in relationship, the law will always be there to help you if you or your beloved partner is a victim of domestic violence. Then you or your partner who is a participant in this violence cannot escape by saying that I am not married at all, so what domestic violence?

If you are spending your time with your future husband or wife in live-in and suddenly one day he behaves like an anti-social element of the society instead of your future life partner, that is, he has given you physical or mental pain, and You have been exploited in this way and you have now realized that he is not worth having an unbreakable bond of marriage with me. So you can complain about it by going to the nearest police station. After this, the police will try to get your future life partner punished under domestic violence along with wiping your tears.

Some important observations of the High Courts of India related to "live-in relationship".

1. Punjab and Haryana High Court, while ruling on an issue, has said that live-in relationship is not illegal. There is no word wife anywhere in the Domestic Violence Act and this case, the female partner is also eligible for protection and maintenance.

2. Similarly, if there is talk of the right of a child born in live-in relation without planning and without desire, then for that the Kerala High Court has said that the child born in a live-in relationship will be treated as the child of the married couple. The bench said that the main object of the law is the restoration and protection of a child in need of care and protection. The right of reinstatement rests first with the parents, then the adoptive parents, foster parents, guardians and finally the appropriate persons. Keeping in mind that a live-in partner has a right to reinstatement, the court in its judgment held that the biological parent's right to be a parent is a natural right.

3. In this interesting anecdote, it would be correct to say another anecdote or law that if a couple is living in a live-in relation for a long time, then the court will see it as a marriage. If you want to avoid the charge of marriage made by the court, then it will be entirely up to you what evidence you present in the court which can convince the court that you are not married.

In the end, the important point of this story is that if you think that before going into a complicated and responsible relationship like marriage, we should understand each other by staying live-in, Whether we deserve that long-lasting relationship with each other or not is just a flurry of hormones in our bodies.

TWENTY-THREE

THESE THREE MONKEYS ARE VERY IMPORTANT FOR ANY RELATIONSHIP TO LIVE WELL.

You must have heard about the Father of the Nation Mahatma Gandhi, if you have not heard, then first you check your passport or look at the identity card of your country, what is written in the column of nationality in it? If it proves that you are Indian, then quickly look at your Indian money. You will remember all about Gandhiji.

If you think of the great man Gandhiji, then with him his useful thoughts of life will also start flowing in your mind. One of those ideas is his beautiful idea related to his three monkeys, whose story is included in the childhood memory of every Indian. When during school days we were given a unique lesson through our lovely teachers, which was very interesting. Which we were always eager to hear. Because the way of saying that brilliant idea was different. Because of that manner, our attention was repeatedly drawn to the person who said that thought

But after knowing about these monkeys, do not start thinking that Gandhiji had raised three monkeys. To whom Gandhiji used to feed bananas by sitting on his lap every day. No, it is not so, but it is in the form of Gandhiji's unique monkey statues, which are believed to reach Bapu through China. People from all over the country and abroad often used to come to Mahatma Gandhi for advice. During the same consultation, people used to give him some gifts in his honour. In the same gifts, these three monkeys are also included.

One day a Chinese delegation came to meet him. After the conversation, they gave a gift to Gandhi Ji and said that it is not bigger than a child's toy but is very famous in our country. Gandhiji was very happy to see the set of three monkeys. He kept it with him and kept it for the rest of his life. In this way, these three monkeys were associated with his name forever.

So what was that monkey idea which is very interesting and which gives us the biggest lesson of life?

It is believed that these monkeys represent the principles of do not see evil, hear no evil, speak no evil and also have cute names of monkeys who show this principle. In which the name of the first monkey is Mizaru, the second is Kikazaru and the third is Iwazaru.

Mizaru Monkey:

It has closed its eyes with both hands. Not because he is shy, but because he wants to close his eyes and tell us that we should not see anything bad. Now here comes the question, what should we not see bad? For how long do we have to keep our eyes closed? Or where should you go and close your eyes?

When Mizaru closes his eyes and indicates that we should not see anything bad, he also expects you to use your common sense. Because there is a lot of bad and good too in this world, so we cannot keep our eyes closed all the time and the second argument our brain also gives us is that when we do not have any understanding of bad, then how can we consider someone good. When you know that intoxication is a bad thing and drinking milk is very beneficial for health, then by recognizing this difference, you can easily choose that milk for yourself, as long as you want to maintain your health. That's all Mizaru monkey wants to tell by closing his eyes.

Kikazaru Monkey:

He has closed his ears with both hands, that is, one who does not hear bad, but he has heard very bad in the early part of life, And now through his understanding, he has chosen this method to live his future life in a better way. He has understood that any bad words of any kind cannot help me to move forward in my life.

Ivazaru Monkey:

He has kept his mouth closed with both hands, which means he has turned out to be smarter than the three monkeys, Because he has come to know which part he has to use in reality, in what way and when. This monkey wants to teach it by closing its mouth that it does not matter that you have seen something bad, it does not matter that you have heard something bad, But if you include the bad that you have heard and the bad you have seen in your life experiments, then not you but your life will become bad for you. If you want to keep your life wonderful and always want to be successful on every occasion, then always speak well, reduce your anger and keep doing good work.

Now after taking so many sermons from these lovely monkeys, your question would be that the title of this chapter was going to take us to the world of relationships, suddenly where did Gandhiji's three monkeys come from?

These three monkeys were not brought suddenly, but I want to show here that to have a better life, to appear as a good person and to achieve sincere success, it is necessary to adopt the gestures of these monkeys. You need a lot.

Similarly, to keep the relationship related to you alive, there are three other monkeys, who will tell in the gestures how you have to maintain your relationships with love for a lifetime.

In the episode of these monkeys, there is also a cute name of monkeys who give knowledge of relationships, which have not been printed in the pages of any history but have been made by me on an imaginary point. In which the first monkey's name is Sunaru, the second is Samjhanu and the third is Samjaru.

So let's hunt the first monkey Sunaru, but not for food nor to sell his skin at good prices, but to learn from him what to do to handle any relationship with love for a long time.

Sunaru Monkey:

Sunaru the monkey keeps his hands on his ears while sharing his knowledge related to relationships, but here he does not close his ears like Gandhiji's monkey but just touches his ears and tries to tell us that, Listening is also very important in a relationship. The person who has mastered this process can never fail in any relationship of his life. Because every person wants to say something, there is a huge shortage in the number of listeners.

Because the listening people have become so mean in this mean world that they only listen to those people who get these three reasons.

1. Greed
2. Fear
3. Authority

If a person comes to know that I am getting benefit by listening to a person of this name, maybe that benefit is related to money or is related to some need of the body, which satisfies the psychological thirst of a person. Or hearing anything from a person may satisfy his physical need. If a person is listening to any other person for his greed, then his greed will not be visible when that person is indulging in the act of listening to another person. This greed is known only when the person through whom the greed of that greedy person has been fulfilled if he tries to identify that greed or there can be a third person, who keeps a sharp eye on these two persons.

It might be that the words "first person, second person" might have made you a little uncomfortable. That's why I like fictional stories to understand the aspects of real life, which are commonly known as examples in the world. So we can also resort to a fictional story to understand these

"Reasons To Hear".

Part One: Mukesh, his boss and his family's tangle

There is a person named Mukesh who works in a big corporate office. This means that he has a fixed time to go to the office and come home and also it means that he will have a boss who is specially meant to keep an eye on Mukesh and people like Mukesh, that these people are doing their work properly during office hours or staring at a beautiful girl on their PC. The job of this boss is that whatever work he has got as the target of his company, he gets that work completed on time by his subordinates. For this, this boss keeps on using weapons like fear, greed and authority on people working like Mukesh according to time.

One day when Bose comes to Mukesh he sees Mukesh with a very sweet smile. Mukesh also gets in a state of surprise for a while that till today the boss who used to stare at me, why is he smiling so much suddenly seeing me today? When the boss lovingly told Mukesh the reason for his smile, Mukesh returned to his normal posture. The reason was that his boss has given him a task which was doing the work to increase the burden on the rest of Mukesh's work. His boss gave this greed to Mukesh and said that I know that this work is not yours. You are already sitting with a lot of office work on your shoulders, and because of this work, you will have to work twice as hard and give twice your time. But if you do this work then you will get a good bonus next month along with your salary and with this, your chances of getting a promotion will also increase. Hearing so many beautiful things from his boss' mouth, Mukesh immediately said yes.

After this, the same moments always pass in Mukesh's office, but this time Mukesh had to spend more time in his office. Tired Mukesh went to his house. He Quickly threw his office bag in some corner of the house and took off all his clothes and lay down on the sofa. His children shouted papa-papa and started demanding things of their childhood from Mukesh. His wife started telling him about her day with a glass of water. But Mukesh was so tired that even though he had ears, he could not hear anything in them. The children and his wife felt pity for Mukesh's face and decided to voice their demands and views the next morning. The next morning also Mukesh did not hear anything nor pretended to hear anything and said that I have a lot of work, I will not listen to anything now. Whatever you want, wherever you want to go and whatever you have to say, I will listen to everything next week. Excuse me for now.

The moral of the story:

Why was Mukesh here listening attentively to his boss? Whereas his boss was not praising him, but with Mukesh's regular cumbersome work and giving extra work to Mukesh. Even then Mukesh was listening carefully to his boss, why? Here Mukesh could stop talking to his boss and tell him the condition of his cumbersome work and say that he cannot do extra work now. Already I am sitting with a lot of work. But Mukesh did not do this, because his boss had shown him dreams of a good bonus and promotion in a big cabin. In the greed of fulfilling those dreams, Mukesh listened to all the things of his boss until his boss left after finishing his talk.

And on the other hand, when his family goes to Mukesh to narrate anything, Mukesh refuses to listen to them all. Because no greed of Mukesh is being fulfilled by listening to his family. So this proves that Mukesh was following the rule of listening in this story because the reason behind Mukesh's greed was hidden behind him.

Part Two: Mukesh, his boss and his family's tangle

A large part of Mukesh's life was on the behest of his boss and because of that large part, his remaining part was also not according to his mind. In the life of this boss's gestures, Mukesh was doing the extra work given by his boss. Many days had passed, so Mukesh's boss again comes to Mukesh and inquires about his condition, not for Mukesh but for the work he had given to Mukesh. When the boss came to know that Mukesh has not done that extra work and still it may take a long time to do that work, then because of this situation, the boss changed his attitude a lot. That is when the boss was talking sweetly to Mukesh to get his work done, Now that Bose was scaring Mukesh by reminding him of the bad consequences of the future. Bose tells Mukesh that if you do not complete this work in the coming two days, Your bonus and promotion will not only go from your hands, but your job may also be in danger with it.

Because of this fear, Mukesh again reached home late today. Then the same drama that was left, started happening. The children again started crying for not fulfilling their demands and his wife wanted to tell the condition of her life to Mukesh, she was also standing in the queue with a glass of water for Mukesh. Thinking that today Mukesh will listen to them. But Mukesh again entangled his family in excuses and, giving some other time of the day, moved towards his bed from there.

The moral of the story:

What was the reason that Mukesh listens to his boss this time too, but not to his family? That is the fear of losing his job, due to which Mukesh listened carefully to his boss's priceless thoughts and started to follow them. But when it came to the turn of the people of Mukesh's family, Mukesh had no fear. Then he used to believe that even if I do not listen to my family, they will remain with me.

Part Three: Mukesh, his boss and his family's tangle

One day Mukesh was immersed in his work like normal days. His boss comes to Mukesh and invites him to his son's birthday party at his house. Asks him to come on time and in the meantime, he starts narrating his son's pranks and cute tales. Mukesh speaks nothing in the middle and listens to all those things very carefully. Mukesh listened to the stories of his boss's son from diaper changing to rod accident, in which Mukesh was not interested. Still, Mukesh was listening to the story of his boss's son as if he was listening to the story of his son.

After the completion of these stories and work from his office, Mukesh goes to his house. But today his children and wife welcome Mukesh at home not with love but with great anger. Because Mukesh does not take out any time for his family, that is, in simple words, he does not listen to his family, that is why there is a fight between his wife and Mukesh, in which his children play the role of spectator. Mukesh's wife had been harbouring anger for not being able to express all the things inside her for a long time, today only she had got a chance, which she used quite rightly for herself. Mukesh's wife was going on speaking in anger but Mukesh did not remain silent here as he remains silent on any bad thing of his boss. Mukesh started speaking more than his wife here and in anger, he started using words to increase that quarrel. The result of which was that Mukesh did not get anything to eat that day. Because Mukesh does not know how to cook and the one who knew how to cook, that is, his wife, got angry and went to the house of a neighbour friend.

The moral of the story:

What was the reason that Mukesh listened to the story of his boss's son, that too in which Mukesh was not interested, even then Mukesh calmly adopted every word of his boss with his ears. But when the turn of his family came, in which now his relationship was at stake. Even then, Mukesh did not listen to a single word of his family calmly, on the contrary, he gifted many bad words in return. So this shows that Mukesh had an authoritative reason to listen to his boss, because of which he knew that this person is my officer, who is more capable than me. If I don't keep good behaviour with him then my job may be in danger. This is the reason Mukesh did not see in his family, while he should have listened to his family with the same level as he was listening to his boss.

Most of you are like Mukesh, who tries to find out these three reasons behind anyone listening to anything calmly. If you get one of these reasons, then you will pretend to listen to that person from the heart, but if you do not get it, then you will have your own family, even then you will not listen to them. Because you think that it does not matter if I do not pay attention to any matter of my family, still they will remain with me. It's not like that at all. When relationships start to deteriorate, you have to listen to them to handle them too. If you do not listen even at that time, then the relationship gets worse and there comes a time that someone dear to you has gone away from you, And it goes so far from you that even if you are ready to listen to him now, he will not come to tell you his words.

Therefore, in time, keep listening to all your relationships, which you want to keep with you until their talk is over. This will increase his love and respect for you, and whenever you are at home, its environment will be many times better than any other place in this world.

Samjhanu Monkey:

Samjhanu monkey, touching his brain, wants to tell that your work is not finished just by listening. You are not listening to a rock song, which is more important for you to enjoy that song than to understand it and even more than the lyrics of a rock song, many people like the music used behind it, the music that even the lazy person would start shaking his hands and feet after listening to it. If you hear such words, then it is a matter of joy, but when it comes to relationships, such relationships are very close to you and you also want to keep them close to you at all times. So just listening to all the things about such relationships will not work. You also have to understand them. You will also have to use your intelligence on them. Just like listening to what your relationships want from you will not work, you also have to know its importance. Can he get what he wants in the true sense or is it just his illusion?

If your father is choosing a career of his choice for you, then you have to understand on this whether you are able to feel comfortable with that career option or not? Can you achieve any position in your life through this career or do you already have a chosen path due to which you cannot follow the path shown by your father?

Can the life partner be chosen by your mother to play the role of your life partner for you or not? If not, then by understanding your mother's words, you can give her a reason for not following her words. Refusing outright just by listening may make them feel bad, but if you listen to them and understand them and then put your thoughts in front of them, she will also get a kind of comfort that my son or daughter has completely listened to me and understood.

After listening completely to your life partner who wants to talk to you, you have to understand from her words how she sees her married life and how do you see your marriage? Is her thinking very different from yours and if different then how can you adjust yourself with that different thinking? You can understand this thing only by listening to all kinds of thoughts of your life partner. If every time you cut your life partner's talk in the middle or what he said, you only included it in your listening and did not understand what was the meaning of those things? Then your relationship will be only for a few years in this era, where the ratio of the person to suffer any kind of trouble has become much less than before.

What do your children want? What do your friends want? What do your neighbours want? What do all your relatives want? The ones you want to have with you. Listening carefully to their words and understanding them makes your relationship even stronger.

Because you take relationships very lightly. The way you do the rest of your life and the importance you give to them while doing them, you do not give as much importance to your relationships. Because here your concept of "Gain And Lose Taste" goes on.

As you got the fever of love for the first time in your life, then the zeal that you used to appreciate your partner, does not remain in you after achieving that partner completely. Because you have fulfilled all your needs like physical, psychological, economic and social needs through your partner, And you must have guessed that now I do not need to make as much effort as I used to do to appreciate my partner before marriage.

It's the same as you used to remember every day your desire to visit some wonderful place for a long time. Used to admire all its beautiful photos many times a day. To reach there, you used to see the figures of your savings again and again, whether there have been enough savings so that I can go to the place of my years' old wish or not. The day when your time comes when you are ready to go to your favourite place physically, mentally and financially, on that day your enthusiasm, your happiness and the perspective of looking at your life at a different level, And when you have reached that place, you have felt every moment of it with your heart. Then after that, your enthusiasm for that place and that happiness of yours does not last to the level it was on the day you were ready to go there.

You unknowingly apply this notion to all your other relationships as well. You think that these people are always with me, no matter how I behave with these people, even then it will not make any difference to them. This is your biggest illusion. No relationship is run by the notion of "Gain And Lose Taste". If so, then this is the reason for breaking many relationships in today's era, because none of your relationships gives you pleasure in the same way. Many aspects of happiness come in front of you with time and many times you have to find a means to get different types of happiness for that relationship with your efforts. So that you can fill a new type of taste in your boring relationship again.

But it is also true that with every joy and with every happiness, a sad situation is waiting for you, which you will have to face. So if you want to keep any of your relationships with love for a long time, then there must be continuity in your efforts, which can always fill your relationship with enthusiasm, happiness and lots of appreciation for each other. You have to always appreciate your relationships and the way to do that is to first listen calmly to them and second is to understand what they have given their views.

Samjaru Monkey:

Now has come that monkey who will give you a chance to speak, that is, Samjaru, who, pointing to his mouth and brain, says that after listening completely to the things of your relationship, understand those things completely. After that comes your time. Now it's your turn to present your case. Now it's your turn to speak and your relationship's turn to listen.

Now after this your question may be that after reading this chapter of this book, we have understood the importance of listening and understanding, but will our relationships also follow this rule which you have told?

It will work, not because they have also bought my book, but after giving your enough time to all the things about those relationships and after the satisfaction that your relationships got from your time, they will stop speaking on their own, and they will sit in the prepared posture to hear your words.

Because it is a matter to think that why does a person start shouting while speaking? Because of all the people in front of whom that person puts his point of view, those people were ignoring him for a long time. No one was giving him any attention, especially his works which he wants to get done by speaking to those people. When he gets an idea that these people are not listening to me, then that person gets angry and starts speaking the same things loudly. Otherwise, who enjoys using a lot more energy than other people in normal work. That's why people agitate for different issues, show resentment. So that they can shout their common words in the ears of the deaf government and that government is then forced to listen to those people.

So when you give the satisfaction of listening to your relationships, they will also give you a chance to have your say and this opportunity will be such in which they will listen to you very calmly and carefully. Because you showed your full faith to listen to them. Now you have got a chance to speak from here, but you should not let this opportunity go lightly.

Suppose that someone close to you has to say something to you, then what can he say to you in his act of saying it?

- He can express his wish.
- He can tell any problem of his.
- He can reveal some of his hidden fears to you.
- He may ask you for permission to do some work.
- He can take advice from you on doing the same thing.

- He may ask you for any knowledge related to any subject.
- Someone can tell you his old secret.
- He may share some of his responsibility with you or set up a conversation with you just to enjoy the gossip.

All these goals can be in the conversations you have established with you from your different relationships. So you have to listen to their goals in the same way, then understand them, And then, depending on your situation, the outcome of their goals is to interpret those relationships as your answer.

If someone close to you reveals any of his secrets to you, then it means that you have to keep this secret to yourself, and not make it public, enjoy it in the form of funny things. And the same understanding should apply to you even when someone trusts you and tells their problems. So your duty at that time is that you listen carefully to his problem and if he feels comfortable then you can also give him some good solution for his good. But turning his troubles into jokes and making fun of that person in front of other people, this result shows that your relationship is going to break soon.

There is no point in going deeper now, I know that you have now understood how to maintain your lovely relationship for a long time.

1. The first is to listen calmly to all that they have to say.
2. The second is to understand all their points carefully.
3. Third, when the time comes for you to speak, identify the real goal of that conversation and present your answer to them.

> "*If you follow these three important rules sequentially, then in any of your relationships, love will take the place of arguments, quarrels and many wrong words.*"

- But one more thing is to use these rules sequentially in your relationships. If you have used any of the rules before, then using and not using these rules will be equal, and your relationship may get worse.

Part Five: All About the "Work".

Now you have to take a dip in those rivers of knowledge, in which you will learn that how can you learn whatever work you have to do in your life? From whom to learn? How can you know the extent of knowledge imparting to the one who is teaching you? And what you've learned so far, have you understood it correctly or are pretending to understand it, how to find out? And how does any work begin?

TWENTY-FOUR

HOW TO LEARN ANY WORK?

Many times you must have looked in the internet world to find the answer to this question that,

- How do I learn this work or how do I learn that work?
- How can I learn the work that my boss wants me to do?
- How to learn the work that removes my unemployment
- How to learn the work that attracts a particular person
- What path should I try to follow to improve my passion work?

So that I can present the highest result till date in that work or can just fill the demand of time, which is asking me to learn that work at the moment? Most of the time you get from this internet world or from a particular person or some organization which claims to teach you the work you want, through which you follow those external steps so that you can learn only that certain work. This external step which is a method made through an internet website, or under the guidance of a particular person or by a certain organization, by following which honestly, you can learn only that work, which you want to learn

Just like you have to learn the computer program Microsoft Excel, so that you do not turn your hair white in doing paper calculations and handling those things more than that. Therefore, with this modern era, side by side, by applying today's methods of accounting in your business or professional work, you can identify the plight of your work in the form of data during your work time. To learn this program, you sat down in a computer chair at the institution of a Joker computer course. Now you are being told the rules and formulas to learn that excel through a teacher and you are learning them daily according to your mental capacity. But the thing to note here is that you are only learning the program of that excel, and you are not concentrating your attention on any work.

Now your funny answer will be that if I want to learn Excel then why should I concentrate on any other work? That's right, your attention should be completely focused on what you want to learn. Only then will you be able to be the best in it. But I am not motivating you here to divert attention from your work. Rather, I am trying to take you towards that secret, knowing that secret will make you the best in everything that you want to learn.

Your basic nature is that you try to follow the same rules, which have been bothering you in recent times. If that problem is not there in your life now, then you will not spend your time in any preparation to face it, unless that problem compels you so much that you have to face it in the end. So what would happen in such a situation?

It will be the same, as a boxer had challenged you to kill inside a ring six months ago today. You told that boxer the excuse of not being prepared enough to avert that dangerous moment. He took pity on you, decided to break your back after six months, and you ran away happy then. Thinking that I got rid of this problem. You played with your precious time of that six months, neither did you think of learning your boxing nor did you pay attention to your fitness. On the contrary, after six months your condition becomes like this, you should not stand in front of any boxer. Rather you need to stand in front of a doctor. So in the end it happened that the boxer punched your growing belly. Your game is over, your girlfriend is unfaithful to you and becomes that boxer's girlfriend, And what you needed doctor before this game, your need is fulfilled after this game is over.

So what did you learn from this combat fiction story? That you should learn those things in time, over which your control is only for some time. After that, you give your control to the result of your work. If you have learned that job well, followed its rules effectively and have paid special attention to your shortcomings in that work. Then according to the control of the result of your work, sweet fruits of good quality will be presented in front of you. Otherwise, the result of your work will force you to put bitter expensive medicines in your mouth.

So here the question should be of your curiosity that by following which rules can I learn any work effectively? Not that you just ran after the ways to learn that particular job.

That is necessary but before that, it is important that the measures which I have to learn, how can I learn them to their highest level? To do your best in that learning process, you need to go through three paths.

1. Time:

After reading this, do not start looking at the time in your watch, come on, today I have acquired a lot of knowledge. I do something exciting except this book. In response to this attitude of yours, I would say that the story has just started and the work of learning will continue throughout life, only the medium changes but there is so much to learn in this life that you have to borrow one more life. So on this basis, you have a lot to learn and very little time for this, so keep learning.

And as far as this first path is concerned, whose title is time, that time does not define the time of life, but everything that you want to learn in that life, this title is related to the time of learning.

It is a very simple way that if you want to learn any work, then you have to take a special time for it. Special time means the time in your day in which you give only for learning your desired work. In that time, you should not have goals set for doing any other work.

Now after reading this, your mind will come to the revolt that I had spent my time and money on this book for these common-sense things?

- Yes, because you also know that you should be honest in your life.
- Because you also know that where you live, the responsibility of the cleanliness of that place is equally shared with you along with the government systems.
- Because you also know that paying your income tax on time comes in your true patriotism.
- Because you also know that you should not indulge in activities that give rise to any kind of discrimination.

Yet over time, through different mediums and forms, you read, hear, see and feel these good things again and again, yet you fail to do these good things whether you want or not. Because it also comes in the lesson of our basic human nature that we quickly learn dirty talk, thought, thinking, nature and many other dirty deeds and start trying what we have learned in our ways of living. For this, we do not need to see, hear, read and feel any dirty environment again and again. In a single effort by us, we become the best student in that dirty environment.

And the same if you look at the good, no matter what kind it is, no matter how effectively it is presented, no matter how much effort is hidden behind the person who brings that good, no matter what the value of that good. Even if there is no value fixed to do good to the people, even then the medium of goodness will not be able to make the same effect on the people as it is initially expected.

So when you have come to know those good things are good to read-only, but when it comes to using those good things in reality, then you forget them or pretend to forget them. To put an end to this drama, you constantly indulge yourself in acquiring such knowledge, so that with it you keep awake that necessary goodness in yourself so that your belief of being a human remains in yourself.

So to maintain this feeling, we come to the title of our time, in which the first issue comes that for whatever work you want to learn, you have to take a fixed time out of 24 hours of your day every day. Because you have already been beaten by a boxer above. In which you feel that because of that boxer you had to visit a doctor, while that boxer was not at fault. It was your fault that you were not able to use your time properly. Therefore, for whatever work you want to learn, you will have to sacrifice some part of your days on your learning activities.

Now let's assume from here that you have become very excited after reading all these motivational things, so much so that you are now ready to sacrifice some time out of your every day. So will this sacrifice of yours fulfil your own learning goal? No, as long as you don't turn the car of your desires on this other path.

2. Concentration:

Is this concentration to be mixed with time to make a sweet pickle? If not, then what is the point of following this path? Its meaning is so important that the time taken by you to learn any of your work will go down the drain in vain if you do not try to walk on this path along with the path of that time.

Because having a focused path in your learning proves that you are making good use of that time. If you try to find more description of the way of this concentration, then you will find that such a situation is born in your learning process, while doing the action in your mind only thoughts related to that action should come and other than that you should not get any other idea. Don't even think about the subject, even if that topic is more important than your learning process. If any other topic related idea comes to your mind at that time, then without focusing too much on it, you should immediately throw yourself into your prescribed learning activity. So that during that learning process you are exposed to all the aspects of that work.

In learning that work, you must have read, seen, heard or written every single rule of it. When, through these physical and mental activities, you acquire the knowledge of learning a task, then its state is called concentration. And by going through such a situation, you do not need to stress your brain too much to remember those learned things. In a few moments, a recorded video of all those learned things starts playing in your mind.

It is as if you and some of your friends decided to go to some hidden mysterious beautiful place. Now the idea of going there was yours, so it was your responsibility to remember its paths. When you were going to that beautiful place, there were many forests around in which it is very difficult to find the paths in general. You made this difficulty even more and you spent that whole path having fun with your friends. That's how you reached that place. There you captured your very special moments on your camera. Running, falling, letting go and you did a lot of body tiring activities. But when it came to going back, all eyes were on you. Because the responsibility of taking everyone back home was on you. Because you only had to remember the paths on which you reached that beautiful place.

Now it has happened that your mind has deceived you after going a little way. You can't remember anything now. Your amnesia was known to your friends from your face without you informing and your friends beat you fiercely in anger, yet you could not remember the way home.

Now, who could help you with this story? Your concentration, if you were concentrated at that time and looked at those paths, then you probably would not have been beaten up by your friends. That's why concentration is necessary for every work that you want to learn, otherwise without it that time is just passed for you, it is not used.

So now you have fully understood the secret that is needed to do any work. No, there is still one way left, on which walking further refine your learning goal.

3. *Hard work:*

What is refinement? Before you refine any work, isn't that work, isn't it? It's work. It is as if a goldsmith has a large amount of gold lying with him, yet no woman has attacked that gold through her purchases. Why so? Because the quantity of gold does not matter whether that goldsmith has a lot of gold lying with him, as long as that gold has not been moulded into some beautiful jewellery, necklace or some attractive ring. If that gold has not been used in such wearables. If that gold had not been heated by a craftsman to give birth to such an attractive art, seeing that everyone would be inclined to take it. All these works are called refinement, in which one has to present an already existing work to its best level in its way. So that the number of people who give importance to that work becomes huge. Praise him and most importantly, the real reason behind learning is that work by you should accomplish the goal in a very good way.

So what needs to be done to adopt the quality of refinement? That is hard work. It does not matter how good you are, how intelligent you are, and how quickly you can learn new things. Unless you do that work again and again with your effort, that work will not present in the way you wanted on the day of its result.

The clear meaning of working hard is to try again and again, the path by which you have to reach your destination one day, you have to pass through that path so many times that every single thing on that path must be sitting in your mind. What kind of trees are there on that road, what kind of trees are there on which curve? Where does the town start? What is the way to avoid dangerous animals? Which would be the safest place to stay the night? What are some tricks to try on a sudden event? From where will the food arrangements be made? You have to pay close attention to each work, due to which you cross that path and reach your destination safely and smoothly.

So just discovered that secret, because of which you can do any work, no matter how difficult it is, you can learn it and one day you can make a different identity with the same work. You have to use these spices not only according to your taste but according to the real demand of your work.

Now after travelling this far, perhaps your mind must have come in a logical state, and its logical question would be that you have not added interest factor in this series of mysteries? So my answer to this logical question is that I have not forgotten to add the factor of choice to it, but it is a matter of thinking that if there is some work which you like to do, So while doing that work, you will not need to remember these three paths. You will naturally start walking on these paths, on the contrary, you will put more effort than any other person to do the work of your choice.

These paths are made for those who want to learn some of their work, but they have never faced that work. So it is obvious that that work will not be of their choice and yet that person will either learn that work by following these three paths or will do that work.

TWENTY-FIVE

FROM WHOM SHOULD YOU ACQUIRE KNOWLEDGE OF THE WORK YOU WANT TO DO?

You know that how you have to learn any work. But should you have a chance to choose the work you want to learn, whatever it may be, to learn it. And every time in doing every work, in giving your support or opposition to every sentiment, in making every plan successful or unsuccessful, in choosing an honest or dishonest side in every work, With every thought, you have a chance to make a choice. Why do you get a chance to choose? What happens with any election? It is a simple matter, choice is such a medium, by adopting the use of which you find the best of your desire, feeling, object, service and any group of people.

What is the importance of having elections in a country like India? Which plays the role of the largest democratic country in the world. Where the public should know this important thing that there is no one in their country bigger than them, they have many opportunities to prove this, which are in the form of various types of election programs. Where the public decides who is the greatest and who is the slave of whom. But the realization of this priceless thing is explained by the leaders of the people here, that too through their attractive speeches during the election days.

Not because the leaders here always think in the interest of the public, but because they do such awareness work so that the people of India can assess their speeches (not their actions) and decide that this leader how good is. How much does this leader care for us? This leader is capable of the development of this country and our development. I will give my vote to this only.

If you feel good listening to someone's speech, you have been impressed by it, then the way to appreciate it is not to make that person your leader, who will take decisions for you later. If a person's speech was good, then it clearly means that that person is better than many people in speaking. But whether that person is worthy of becoming your responsible leader or not, it will be known from his past deeds, which he has done in any political position in his past. The work is related to the important issues of your locality or your city or your state or your country. If in the past actions of that person, in his thinking, in his behaviour, if you see such a glimpse that this person is worthy to be my leader, who will not distract me from unnecessary issues like other leaders. Rather, the issues which are necessary for today's time and the issues on which it is necessary to do development work in future, this person will give his utmost efforts to solve those issues. So you should choose that person only. That's why you got the right to vote in an election so that you can give the responsibility of governing on your behalf to anyone leader from a group of leaders.

The same concept of choice is also applicable for acquiring knowledge related to any subject. Even then you have to think that which person or organization will prove to be the best for me, who will give his best in teaching me the work I desire.

What would you do to choose the best one? To learn your work from anyone or take that learned work to the highest level of success, would you take advice from anyone?

- Hey, this is my best friend. He will give me advice with the intention of doing me good.
- Hey, this is my closest relative, I try to get knowledge related to my work from this.
- Hey, this is my richest neighbour, I ask him how can I get ahead in the work I want to do?

The logic here is that if you want to eat ice cream, then you will try to find an ice-cream parlour only. It's not like you'll walk into a tailor's shop to get ice cream and ask him to give you a vanilla-flavoured ice cream. He will not give ice cream but taking pity on your intelligence, will tell you the address of the place where ice cream is actually found.

But our well-wishers, our dear friends, our unbreakable relatives and neighbours like our home, do not show such kindness to us. They are ready to answer any of your questions. These people do not even think that the person who is asking me the question, perhaps the answer will be related to some important decision of his life. If I am not knowledgeable about the subject of that important decision. if I have not decided any path with my efforts in that subject to date, then how can I tell you that what I am telling you is related to that subject, You must believe him.

It is the same thing that you do not know how to swim. You are giving this knowledge to a child that, How can you swim in a big river? That child is also naive, taking your knowledge as the last resort of this world, he jumps into the swing pool near his house. Then next time not he but his parents come to you, that too to praise you with sticks. For the knowledge, you have given to their children.

So the first tip from my side is always taking advice for any work from the one who is knowledgeable of the highest level of that work Or he is doing that work now Or the person you are going to consult for your work, he has already done that work in his life in the past, that too much time of his life has been spent in doing that work. Then that person or any organization, along with their understanding, has the right to give you knowledge through an experience related to that work, And you also have the right to take that knowledge from that person or from that institution about the subject that you want to know.

Because every person's choice, ability and perspective of looking at the world is different, accordingly that person will give his advice, his knowledge or his thoughts in the context of the subject of your curiosity.

Perhaps the counsellor's choice is contrary to yours, then what? So the chances are that that person will describe every possibility related to that subject, which will encourage you not to go ahead on that subject's path. Because from where your stream of knowledge related to that subject is flowing, the source of that stream does not want that stream to flow from the edge of the land of your success and the land of your success becomes fertile. So at that time, negative crops will start growing in your mind too, which till now was cultivating positive for your subject.

Maybe that person has doubts about his ability. Because of this doubt, that person has never tried his hand in the work related to your subject, then such a person will also advise you that you should also not get your hands dirty in that subject. He is indirectly giving birth to dangerous beasts in you to doubt your ability. It is obvious that you will also start looking at that subject from that point of view, and you too will never be able to start anything related to your subject by getting caught in the doubt of this ability.

After reading this, your mind can knock on the door of a question here that being overconfident is also dangerous. Yes, you are right but doubting and thinking logically are two different issues. Doubt shows you a lot of fear in starting any work and fear is there in every work. With such thinking, you cannot start any work.

But thinking logically is like making a map in your mind. Through which you make a great map of decisions related to your subject. Where you know when to start this work related to this subject, how to do it and when I have to decide for its good. And that well-wisher of yours who is far away from your subject does not want to tire his mind so much. That's why he prefers to think more with doubt than to think logically and also advises you to take pills of the same doubt in the morning and evening.

Perhaps your well-wisher's view of this world is completely opposite to yours. Attitude is a thought, due to which a person does the work of his life. If you look from the point of view of a staunchly religious person, then he thinks of giving the title of religion to his religion, he considers other religions as an illusion. So will people of all other religions give up their religion at the behest of that one person? That's impossible. Because everyone has some degree of emotional attachment to their religion. It is impossible to leave at the behest of someone, and at the behest of a person who does not belong to that religion, then it is more difficult.

Religion proves to be beneficial for you only as long as through it you live your life on a moral basis and live within the limits of your country's laws. The day you started violating morality and law, then even if you belong to any of the great religions of this world, still you are wrong as a human being, who deserves a fair punishment.

If the same fanatical religious attitude of the person from whom you are consulting, if he thinks about your subject with the same fanaticism, then the scope of your work will be greatly reduced. The scope of your attainment of knowledge will be reduced. Even before you meet people, an impression will be formed about them, which will prevent you from doing anything new. When the truth of life is that nothing is limited, it is just the rules made by humans. If you want to be successful in your work, then stop setting your limits in advance, on whatever basis it may be.

If still, you consider these ideas as just bookish words, without even knowing their background from any person, which is necessary to match your curiosity, if they do not match. So maybe you will reach your destination, And it may also happen that once you start walking on your destination, after that you get such tremors, after those shocks, maybe you are not ready to think or do something new in the future.

"*It's like gambling, and we've been told from our childhood that gambling is bad.*"

TWENTY-SIX

HOW TO KNOW THE EXTENT OF KNOWLEDGE OF THE PERSON WHO IS GIVING YOU KNOWLEDGE?

- To say at all times that this person or this institution or any person whom you have accepted in your mind as the contractor of knowledge, Is it necessary to call his knowledge right or wrong?
- Can knowledge always be weighed in terms of right and wrong? Why do you think someone's knowledge is correct to your subject and someone else's knowledge is wrong for you?
- Have you ever tried to know the reasons behind it?

These are all such questions, for which your mind can get tired to find a logical answer. I know this. But after searching for the answers to these, you will get a priceless reason to learn anything from anyone, after knowing the reason, your learning will be greatly accelerated in every subject related to this life. Everyone is troubled by the fact that I have less time, but I want to learn a lot, but due to less time, I am not able to learn. So learn from today.

So in order to increase the speed of your learning, first of all, you have to use your mental force to know that, in which I declare my result for any person or organization, whether its knowledge is correct or its knowledge is quite wrong, So does that method work to make my mind aware or does it push me further into the darkness, where there is some light of knowledge. Because of which I am not able to reach my highest level, what should I do for what I want to reach?

When you ask yourself such questions, then your mind gradually becomes of logical nature. He adds links one after the other to the questions asked by you. When all the links are added, you get an answer that comes to a conclusion through using the original part of your brain over a period of time. And that conclusion says that any knowledge related to any person, any subject is not right and wrong, but it is knowledge given on the basis of some kind of limitation. The truth of which is based on all the experiences of the person giving that knowledge. For a person who has knowledge derived from experience, for that person, that knowledge is very close to the truth for that time. But someone else's experience may be greater and different from that of the former.

So what is the experience? Is the passing of a person through the time of his life called experience? No, the definition of experience is your hearing, seeing, speaking, writing, and doing all those things by which you have reached the present time of your life. In which there are many right decisions, wrong decisions and many mistakes, learning from which you do not repeat the same mistakes again. Due to not repeating those mistakes, you are able to take the right decision for different life subjects and after taking that right decision, the result comes in your hands, If you feel satisfied with that result physically and emotionally, then you keep it in your diary of memories as a good experience. So that you can use that good experience to overcome the coming stages in your life and together you can do a social service by sharing those experiences with other people because now those people will not have to go through those mistakes, which you had to go through in your life. But this is possible only when those people use the ideas of that experience in their ways of living. Otherwise, those experiences will be meaningless for those people.

So from this, you learn that a person's experience is the biggest source of his knowledge. On whichever subject you are gaining your knowledge from any person or from some attractive institution, then it may be that he has acquired his knowledge by reading many books on that subject. Or it may be that a person has used the same book things in his life after reading them, And the result that comes out of that experiment, the same result has been described exactly to you.

Perhaps it may be here that out of these two, you should choose the person who did the experiment, in order to know the truth of what he had read, that person has adopted those book things in his life. After that, what he experienced, on the basis of that experience, he is giving knowledge. So in this way, you will believe that the knowledge of this person is closer to the truth.

But it is not a matter of choice in which way you adopt the knowledge of someone else in your life. Rather, the point here is that any knowledge of a person on any subject shall not be declared on the result of whether his knowledge is true or false, but rather on the extent to which he has acquired knowledge in relation to that subject. On that basis, you will make your limit for that person's knowledge.

If you give more priority to the knowledge of experience, then according to that, if a person has had only one book for anyone subject in his life and has used only the rules written in it in his life, And after that the result that comes out, that person tells that result in your ears. But if we look at the other side, then there can also be someone who has read a lot of books. The books which are written on the basis of real experiences, then will you not accept the experienced knowledge of that ocean? Will definitely do it when you come to know about this.

So how does this prove what is the right knowledge and what is wrong knowledge? If it is proved, then only the limits of any knowledge are proved, which is determined on the basis of how much time a person has given to acquire the knowledge of any subject by any means and on what basis.

To understand this more seriously, let's weave a fictional story.

There are two persons, whose subject of work is the same. Both these people fulfil the needs of their life from the business sector and if more income is created then they also fulfil their hobbies. Both these people have been named by their family members on that famous TV ad. Ramesh and Suresh. Ramesh has a successful business empire, whose products have no interest in this story and neither does this story want to know how Ramesh became so successful in his life? Then what is there to know? Want to know what

Suresh does?

Let me tell you that Suresh also has a business but his business is as a shopkeeper. There is no difference between the two, if not much attention is paid to the internal things of their work, then both these people earn their income through business. The only difference is that one person earns a lot of money, and the other earns more satisfaction than money.

One day a person named Mukesh got this itch that I have to do business in my life. Mukesh had thought that now I will not spend my time giving false praise to the boss of any company, but now I myself will become the boss of my business. With this enthusiasm, Mukesh wandered in search of knowledge to make his business dream come true. But this story shows mercy to Mukesh and introduces him to Ramesh, not distracting Mukesh much. This story shows kindness to you too, so instead of talking nonsense, this story tells you those things which are not right for Mukesh but important for you.

That Ramesh is working in his successful business empire, and day and night are trying new ideas, knowledge and experiments in his business methods to grow further. If seen from a glance, Ramesh has spent most of his life building and furthering that successful business.

On the other hand, Suresh has spent a large part of his life in that one shop. Staying within the scope of the same shop, he has worked only on acquiring and applying the knowledge related to it, to complete all the works related to it.

The point to be noted here is that there is nothing right and wrong in the knowledge of these two, the only difference is the extent of that knowledge, in which Ramesh is working at the highest level of business, which includes Retail, Wholesale, Marketing, Peking. , distributing, customer satisfaction, customer reviews and many more business parts on which Ramesh is working. If Mukesh will gain knowledge from Ramesh, then he will get to know the nuances of all these businesses and the knowledge which is meaningful is of use only if Mukesh also intends to start the same level of business.

And the same if Mukesh takes his "Knowledge Bowl" to Suresh, where he meets a man who knows everything about a retail shop. He knows that by taking which type of goods from which market, he can get a good margin of profit. He has experience in dealing with different types of customers. He knows that he has to keep the goods that make the customer happy and satisfied at his shop so that by selling them in time, he can make a great income for his month.

Now you tell me on what basis you will weigh the knowledge of these two, you cannot say right or wrong. You can just set a limit that Ramesh keeps the knowledge of running a big company and Suresh keeps the knowledge of running a shop in a great way.

TWENTY-SEVEN

HAVE YOU UNDERSTOOD WHAT YOU HAVE LEARNED IN THE RIGHT SENSE OR ARE YOU PRETENDING TO UNDERSTAND IT?

Do you know why people spend a lot of their time and money on making idols? But before this, the question comes that why do people make idols? It is obvious that any group of people who are spending a lot of their time and money behind making an idol, that too except for other painful issues, especially that it is done in huge quantity by the leaders of the country of India. If so, then there must be some reason behind making those idols. Otherwise, why would any leader or people who voted for that leader want that a leader should spend a lot of money and useful time of this country on making that statue, And, while many important issues are yet to be resolved in this country, which requires a lot of money and time along with mental ability. Still, why such hard work behind making an idol of a god or a great man instead of those important issues?

- Was there not a single idol of those great men before this? No, it is not so. Even before, many idols are present of many great men.

- Was it not able to recognize by looking at the earlier idols, whose idol it is? No, it is not like that either. People recognize by looking from afar.
- Then what do we want to prove by making such a high and expensive idol?

Actually, it is nothing, the leaders of India and the people who voted for those leaders have read the wrong definition of respect. What about the idol and the respect? It is only then that idols are made. How? So for this, first of all, it has to be understood that when any person is given the status of God or great man?

When that person, apart from the common people, has sacrificed his life for the betterment of the entire human society, for their development, to make the future beautiful and through his thoughts, worked on different subjects, in different forms. Yes, whose great thoughts and deeds become impossible for a generation to forget, then that generation gives that person the status of God or great man, And by preparing this status as a special day, that generation gives its blessings to the next generation. When that special day of such a great man comes, then those people who believe in that great man, respect him on that day.

Even that is fine, they should be respected. But if one wants to respect a great man or God, then it is necessary to make his idols. Will he be respected in this way? If this is the only way, is it correct?

Here the question has not been raised on any great man or on any God. Rather, questions have been raised on you and your ways of honouring a great man. Have you ever thought that if you spend so much time and money in making idols of great men and Gods, then what if those great men and God were in your midst today, So would that great man and God be happy to see your way of honouring this?

Of course not. Now you will think that all those great men have come to my ear and said all this? No, but I have a logical answer to it. Which will satisfy you completely. If still you are not satisfied then you are not, the thought sitting in your mind which is related to your way of respecting a great man, is very stubborn, which does not go from your mind.

Come on, I try, maybe that stubborn idea of yours goes away.

What is the reason that you put an idol of any great man? So you would say on this that that is the reason, to respect them. So I ask here that why do you respect any great man? Because those great men had spent their whole life in the contemplation of doing good to the entire human race, leaving their own interests. The views of those people were of a much higher standard than the views of the common people. The way of life of those people was full of good things. That is why you are impressed by the good qualities of those people and consider them as great men. That's why you remember those people even today. That's why you respect those people even today. So I ask you again that the purpose of respect is fulfilled only by making an idol? This is your biggest illusion and you know it but still do not want to remove this illusion.

If you want to respect any great man, then try to adapt his thoughts to your life. Taking lessons from their good deeds, incorporate those deeds into the real purpose of your life. Try to learn their good qualities, because of which they are known. Only then will they be really respected and only then can we do our full development with these methods of respect.

So what do you enjoy in respecting someone in whom respect is a sham? But that respect is of no use to your life. If you want to respect someone, then respect in such a way that along with you, the people of your group are also benefited. And while doing that good deed, the name of that great man will also continue from generation to generation with respect.

But what is truth? Do you know? That you know all this. You know the manner of this respect but you do not want to play it. Because this way of respect takes a lot of hard work, it takes a lot of effort, the good of someone else is more than your own good and you do not want to live such a life, so a leader chooses the easiest way to show respect. That leader to please the people of a group so that the people of that group make him their leader, That's why by playing with their feelings, he spends a lot of money and time on an idol of a great man believed by them and this money is taken from the tax stock filled by the public. After that those people also become happy, that leader is also happy and then the same leader becomes happy again after winning with huge votes.

So on this concept of respect, your process of learning any work is involved. You go to any resource, to get knowledge about any subject, Or from a particular person when you take knowledge for the subject you are interested in Or reads a book with the aim of incorporating the idea into the way of life, So most of the time your method is to pay respect by making an idol. How? Ask questions, along with your curiosity, your life will also thank you for asking questions. So while answering this question, how is that? So whenever you try to get an idea related to any subject from any source and when you get it, how will you know whether you have understood that idea in the right way or just pretend to understand it. doing?

How? Because if you read millions of books or meet millions of wonderful people or acquire any knowledge from your long experience, whatever it may be, how will you know that you are not just pretending to have that knowledge, Rather, you have understood that knowledge in the right way.

The very simple answer is, if you have used that idea in your life, then you have understood that idea. But if you have not used that idea till now, then you are just pretending to understand that idea or knowledge.

So why do this kind of pretence or why to do this kind of respect which takes a lot of your time and money but it is of no use. With that show in your life, you are not able to develop in any field. So what is the use of doing such a loss, in which you get nothing.

TWENTY-EIGHT
HOW DOES WORK BEGIN?

You have taken a dip in many rivers of knowledge. Now it is time to start your work, remembering what you have learned. Till now you were learning that, how can you learn whatever work you have to do in your life? From whom to learn? How do you know the limits of imparting knowledge to the one who is teaching you? And whatever you have learned so far, have you understood it in the right way or are pretending to understand it, how to find out?

You have solved so many problems related to your life till now. Now it's your turn to work, so now it is to find out how the work you want to start is done from the beginning?

You must have always heard this saying from the mouth of an intellectual that every work starts from a small level. After listening to this, you start saying "yes, this is the right thing" directly in praise of that person. But before praising him, you should think whether this priceless statement of that intelligence is true for all the works of life or not.

This book is not only giving you its precious knowledge related to different types of subjects, but it is also teaching you how to think? Why is it important to think? How to question? Why is it important to ask? If you have noticed that by answering all these questions, this book is trying to make you a creature of logical nature. If this book is doing so much effort for you, then you should also try a little. Be a little logical. Become logical? So let's take advantage of this logic of yours.

Have you ever thought of this priceless statement that how any work can start from a small level, while you have never faced that work till now? For you, that new job cannot be small. When you start any work, which may be of any field or subject, that work is completely new for you. Those who are calling that work small, maybe that work is really small for them because they have met all the nuances of that work. Those people have spent a lot of their time with those nuances. Those nuances also include a lot of mistakes that these "small work" people have come across. They know, how to do this small task? When to try which method? Where is there the most scope for making a mistake and where can I do that small task the best with the help of my ability. Overall, those old people have that experience in which with a lot of time, they have completely adopted that work with all the necessary activities of their body. And when a person adopts any work, then hesitation, fear, embarrassment, such as bad qualities go away from the person's body and that person comes completely at ease with that adopter's work. The person who becomes comfortable does not have to stress much in his physical and mental mediums. For the person who lives in such a comfortable position, the chances of being successful increase.

Now after reading all these scary thoughts, do not understand that I am telling you not to start any work. I never want that. Because people living in these easements must have started their work at some point or the other. These people will also be in the same situation as you are now.

So what is the real purpose of this chapter? So that is that first of all stop saying or understanding that "any work is small". And start saying that every work starts with mistakes, that too many. It does not mean that you can never learn that work or you can never achieve success in doing that work. Don't even think about it, but making mistakes at the beginning of that new work, shows your effort to do that work. Which is very important.

If you make a mistake on the very first day of starting any work, then when you do that work again, will you make the same mistake again? No, not at all. Because you know that I have already fallen on the pit of this mistake, now I do not have to fall again and please the doctors thereby being admitted to a hospital forever.

Whoever is calling your work small, one day you will also start calling the same work small. But before that you should spend your time with that work. After that keep on speaking in front of a new goat, all these arrogant things.

Part Six: Trying to understand an Artist

Take a look at the pages of this part to know the definition of such words like creativity, writer, artist and to be aware of the existence of every artist.

TWENTY-NINE

HOW TO WRITE A BOOK? ARE YOU SUFFERING FROM THIS QUESTION?

Is the question bothering you that how can I write a book? How can I pursue this accolades-robbing and remotely good looking career?

If you are getting this kind of restlessness and you are asking this question to Google God every morning and evening in your beautiful day, then the happy news for you is that your sad days are gone and there is no need to say "happy days". Instead, I will tell you that the days have come for you to face reality.

You will be happy that what I am going to write, everyone can write a book. There is no such evil as discrimination in this capacity. It does not matter whether you are a man or a woman, whether you are black or white, you are a terrorist or an army officer who makes the citizens of a country feel proud. I can claim that you have the ability which is needed to write any book. Because everyone has experienced. Whether it is little or more, bad or good, worth remembering or forgetting, the days of happiness or the evidence of sorrow. Every human being has an ocean of experiences of any kind, related to any one subject or many subjects.

Or it may also be that your experience is related to some profession, as you are in the field of business so far in your life, then you can share your business experiences in that future book. Which may be beneficial for those people who are thinking of making their career in the business field. You can share the experience of love you have found in your life. You can reach a box of your old memories through that future book to the interested people.

Everyone can write a book because everyone has lived and is still living. This means that we all have our series of different types of stories sticking to us, just waiting to put those series in a good title.

After all these motivational things, your next question will be that why I have not been able to write any book till now?

Just as there is a twist in the story of every film that is woven into it to make that film interesting, similarly your desire to write this book has not one but two twists.

The two twists

You have come to know that you can write a book and you also have the wealth of memories that you can fill in that future book. But without doing these two steps, the book you see in your dreams will not come into your hands.

First, Interest:

First of all, you should digest the rule of this nature that every person's interest is different. Everyone's interest is related to different types of subjects. Like someone likes to dance and maybe someone likes to dance only in the marriage of others. Some like to count notes earned from any business, some like to write. It is not necessary for him that if a person has a keen interest in writing, then he has awakened to fulfil the purpose of writing a book. Maybe he writes a blog, maybe he keeps his writing to himself.

If a person has a lot of interest in writing, it does not always mean that he wants to earn money from this field in any way, so that he can spend his life well and His family, friends, relatives and neighbours should stop calling him unemployed. Maybe he can express himself well through this art. With the work of this writing, he can solve all those problems in the depths of his heart, so much that he is not able to do this way through other mediums. eg, laughing, cheering, teasing, shouting, angry And getting into a scuffle with someone in the pursuit of expressing himself evermore. Maybe a person does not feel comfortable expressing himself through these mediums, but he moulds all the things of his mind in a paper in a very good way with the art of his writing.

In the opening words of all this heading, I was talking about that law of nature, which is related to interest, that every person's interest is in different works. After reading this, your mind might be asking the question, what do I have to do with this? You just tell me how can I write a book?

To answer this question, you need to understand this "interest" thing very well.

- Are you interested in some work? You like to do that work and like it so much that even if no one asks you to do it, you start doing that work by borrowing a little time from your life.
- You do not even get the official currency of any country for that work, even then you start doing that work with great pleasure.
- You do not face any kind of problem while doing that work, without stressing your mind too much
- And if you do that work while staying in your natural state, then understand that you are very interested in that work.
- You can thump your chest and say that I like to do this job, fuck everyone.

Think carefully, if you are not interested in this writing field, then it is obvious that you will not even have these above-mentioned things while doing that work. So how can you imagine that you have no interest in writing, even then you want your name written on a thick page book?

For once you will start writing the book of your dreams by keeping this thing written by me on the side. How long do you think you will be able to write? Won't you get bored very soon? How will you think of new and useful ideas to write in that book, until you are in your natural state? Because you will also be aware of this rule that, when we are in trouble, we are sad, angry, and when we are surrounded by the worries of the world, Then your mind stops telling you the ways to get out of that situation.

With this as the basis, try linking it to your book writing activity. When you will not be in your natural posture while doing that work, it means that you are going to be in trouble more or less soon. You are not going to understand anything soon while writing that book. You will forget to use well-descriptive sentences, and later you will come across a situation where you will not feel like writing anything.

All these things do not mean that if any person has to write anything, first of all, ask yourself whether I am interested in writing or not? If you don't get the answer to that question then don't write anything. This is not the meaning of this author, but I am saying this to identify interest and stay in some work for a long time. Because writing a book is not an hour or a day's work, it takes a lot of time. In which has the quality of interest plays a very important role. Because it may be that after seeing a friend, a relative or seeing a book of a famous author getting a lot of attention, you have also felt like writing a book today, but after a few days the same mind will remain, What is its guarantee?

It is impossible without interest unless you copy-paste someone else's writing. Apart from this, you have no choice that if you are not interested in writing, then you cannot produce any book.

Whatever criteria I have set for interest in any subject, if you fit in it, then good luck to you. You are ready to write your book. Now leave this book here and start looking for words that will fit in your book.

Second, Observation:

As everyone has lived life and everyone is living life, This clearly means that everyone has stories and incidents related to different subjects and still all those things are happening with everyone. Everyone is creating new stories every day, directly and indirectly. Everyone has been or is going to go to different types of places. Everyone has met or continues to meet different types of human beings, good or bad, from different cultures, old, children, young, women, beautiful girls, employed, unemployed, unhappy, happy, good thoughts. People with unheard views, people with professional jobs, people thinking about business. And many more people whom you have already met or are about to meet in your future life. With all this, there are different books, videos, movies, sports, so much is there in this life around all of us and so much remains to be seen, heard, spoken, done by you and the people you have met and by the people, you meet in future life.

Now just think, stress your mind. Can't you learn anything from all this? Can't you learn to such an extent that you can write a book from those learned things? You can learn and write your dream book from those learned things. But where is the shortage? Do you know? In your observation, which plays the most important role in writing a book related to any subject.

You don't have to do anything. You just have to look carefully at every little thing and the biggest thing in your life and others' life.

To listen carefully to different things, Any other person and how you do any kind of work, you have to see it. Who's getting angry? And which person is telling how to get rid of anger? Who laughs how and who laughs to hide his sadness? With whom does a person meet and while meeting, does that person remain in his natural posture or keep changing according to different people. You have to see, listen, understand everything carefully and then go and write your thoughts on them using the precious intelligence of your mind. This is the secret of every artist present in the world along with every writer. That's how he executes his every art. Everyone is always learning.

A writer always observes his surroundings and his life closely. That's why a writer can create different, wonderful, useful ideas, stories and anecdotes. Had it not been for this quality, perhaps no one would have been a writer today.

So if you want to become a writer or want to make a book written by your own hands, then, first of all, try to adopt these qualities in your life and after that, you have your understanding. Use it to give birth to a new idea and a new book.

ALL THE BEST..

THIRTY

WHAT IS THE REAL DUTY OF A WRITER?

This question should be asked by every person who reads any type of subject such as self-help, social issues, history, etc.

- Whatever you like, you read an article according to the subject of your desire.
- You read a newspaper for general and current affairs.
- You read the blog of a writer you love.
- You read a book that you think inspires you.
- From what you read, you must ask this question, **What is the real duty of a writer?**

Some of you think that the duty of a writer is to write that topic and to give knowledge about that subject which you want to know, it is the only duty of a writer. No, it is not only the duty of the writer.

Yes, of course, a writer writes on a subject and you read a part of or whole book of that subject but a writer has another important duty to do with the subject that you study and the interesting thing is that you do not know that duty.

Let me tell you the duty which you did not recognize. Countdown begins ... 1..2..3, duty name is Realization.

Yes, it is the real duty of any writer. When you read any type of subject as your wish, there is a writer who drives the car of that subject and you are sitting on the back seat of that car. This means that the entire path of that subject is systematically created by the writer and the writer leads you to that path slowly through your reading and of course through the writer's thoughts to the final stop of that path.

A writer knows how to present words and sentences on any subject that attracts readers and imparts a specific type of knowledge.

But an interesting thing is that an author does not discover new things in an article or a book most of the time.

That means, most of the time you already knew the information that you are going to read and you get such knowledge from self-help books. Most of the time there is nothing new in any self-help book that you do not know. You already know the things that you are going to read, but perhaps you forget those important things or you try to forget that information, so you constantly keep reading such books.

In such a situation, the real duty of any writer is that he passes or fails in making you understand that subject. A writer tries to make his readers feel that the information that you are reading in that book or article, many times you already know, but an author explains that information in such a way that you should also like to read the information and you should also get a realisation for that topic.

For example, I wrote this article on my website about women empowerment.

<u>*"Who is stopping women from becoming independent?"*</u>

I am not going to tell you the meaning of "women empowerment" or essay on it here. You know what is woman empowerment and what is its purpose. If you do not know, you can search for it on the net. There you will find those who explain better than me.

Come on, let me do it for you.

"Paragraph On Women Empowerment – 100 Words for Classes 1, 2, 3 Kids

Women empowerment refers to the activities undertaken to improve women's social, economic, and political status in the world. The female gender has faced subjugation and systematic oppression throughout history, and the situations call for improvement in their condition in society.

Expansion Women empowerment starts with the basic steps of granting women the right to live. To date, thousands of female babies are killed either in the womb or right after their birth. To make sure women are empowered to live their lives freely, female infanticide and foeticide were made punishable by law. In addition to this, women must be educated and given equal opportunities in professional and economic fields."

Have you read it? Now, what next? We have been reading this for years, In school and college, we kept writing essays on it. (Probably to pass an exam) Have been debating this (probably only to win that debate!) Speeches on this will be heard at many social events! Many leaders and social workers have worked on this for many years and still do. What is the problem then? Why are we repeatedly bringing up the same issue? Why do we keep on talking about the same issue again and again? Keep writing, Keep listening, What is the reason for bringing this issue again and again?

According to my, there can be three reasons.

1. Perhaps we are not so intelligent, so we try to understand it again and again.
2. Perhaps it is easier to give a speech or debate on it, therefore.
3. Perhaps we have a shortage of issues.

There is one more reason, and that is our bitter reality. We could not fully implement it.

The issue is not whether we know about it or not? everyone knows, The point is that despite knowing everything, why are we not implementing it in real life. Even today the situation is like that, Our thinking is stuck there too, why? I have the answer.

Two kinds of thinking.

I believe that our two kinds of thinking are hidden behind this issue. We look at it from two angles, so we are not implementing it yet.

- First, the lady of our house.
- Second, the lady from another house.

You must be thinking how is this the view? But this is the view of our bitter truth. Have you ever given someone a SUGGESTION? Often we give. When someone asks, Even if no one asks. And for the person whom we advise, we FORCE that they should implement this advice. You are confident in your SUGGESTION that it is right, Might as well. But you do not trust your advice because it is the right SUGGESTION, but because you believe that even if the advice is wrong, you will not be harmed.

Yes, you INDIRECTLY think in your MIND that my SUGGESTION is absolutely correct and even if it is not correct, what is my loss in it. That's why we are so CONFIDENT while giving SUGGESTION. In the same way, we think of WOMEN EMPOWERMENT. Yes, when you give a speech on this, Your debate on it, You write on it, You become a part of the social program associated with it. Then you do all that for unknown people, Neither of whom you know. Like your relatives, your family. Because you don't want to do this. You want the WOMEN EMPOWERMENT to be applied to someone else's women. It should not be applied to those I know. Like the women in your family.

Otherwise, she will overtake me, She won't listen to me, She will earn more than me, They will be named more than me, She will no longer trust me, She can do everything in her own life on her own, thus she will have confidence in herself. Then what will be my honour? in society? After this, how will I meet people?

Because of all these poor thoughts, two approaches are formed for our WOMEN EMPOWERMENT. The women of our house and women of another house. Think what are we doing?

I had given my views on this issue in this way but this article was not new to you. You already knew all these things but I just made you realize your mistake through my article. I made you realize the activity that still haunts us in implementing women empowerment.

Before reading this article, I reminded you of the important things you had forgotten through this article. I did not offer anything new but gave a piece of information that makes you realize what we are doing wrong.

Is it necessary to realize?

If we read any topic and we do not have any realization of any kind while reading that topic or after reading that topic, then your time is wasted. Because you did not get anything from that subject except such information that you can easily reach it, that too from your phone internet at any time. We should read such things.

But I am not saying that reading any newspaper or reading any information, everything you read is useless. This is not my point of view. This is good for our vocabulary, good for our knowledge of what is happening around us.

But when it comes to life goals or career or anything that we want to achieve in our life, then we should read the kind of information that helps you to reach your goal and you Also realize what you want from your work and life.

- Read what you want to feel.
- Read what motivates you to work.

THIRTY-ONE
WHAT IS THE SECRET OF EVERY ARTIST

How much we enjoy knowing any secret, how excited when we are in the process of knowing any secret and especially when that secret is related to our subject. But, that thing is different that, the happiness of knowing that secret, we are not able to maintain it. What about that, even if any important wish related to our world is fulfilled, still we cannot live our whole life with that one happiness. We constantly need something new. So that our life continues to be filled with enthusiasm. The sooner your destination or desire is likely to be fulfilled, the sooner you will get bored with that achieved or fulfilled desire. The more time you take in the process of achieving the destination or desire, the longer you will be excited, constantly try to indulge yourself in it, will constantly think of new ideas to achieve it, will work hard day and night on it. And when that wish that you wanted for a long time, if you get it, then you will share its happiness with people. But behind that, you do not just think that those people will be happy about your success, but you aim to get more happiness by telling about your success.

Every desire has two states.

The first stage is,

Your time, effort, thoughts, which can be useful and useless in the process before achieving that desire. Using all those ideas in different ways with your intelligence and together with an optimistic thought "I will fulfil this wish of mine in any situation". But the story doesn't end here. If the scary ghost does not come in the way of any of your desires, then understand that that desire is not that important in your eyes or maybe your ability is more than that desire in your mind. Otherwise the scary ghost, that is, with every good thought, a bad idea keeps going along with it in the form of its brother. Whether that bad thought can be seen as a result in your life or not, depends on your giving importance to that bad thought.

But this does not mean that only if you keep thinking good about your desire, then that desire itself will join hands with you. This is just your dream and it will remain a dream. But to make this dream come true, you have to have hard work, better strategy and good thinking. This formula takes you to your desire.

The second stage,

It is felt by you after your desire has been fulfilled. Just like in the time before you got your desire when you used to do new experiments to get that desire, Similarly, to maintain the happiness of the fulfilment of that wish, you constantly try to entertain your heart by trying new ways. In your ways, you try to reach the level of happiness that you were on the day you achieved your age-old wish.

How?

Like you parked such a car in front of your house after working very hard, whose once loud horn made your neighbours face red. Not because you are showing your participation in noise pollution and your neighbours are trying to be aware citizens. Rather, your neighbours have turned red because they are jealous of the expensive car you have bought. But you are no less bad. You would like to see their jealousy towards you with your own eyes by taking a box of sweets to their house very soon in future. After this, you will post such a picture of yourself with that expensive car on social media platforms, on seeing which everyone will say that, I have found the happiest person in the world. (But only you know the reality) Now you will not stop here, to keep the happiness that you have got after so many years, you will have a wonderful party in the joy of buying that car, whose purpose is only to hear the praise of your success from your relatives and neighbours. Then there are other ways to maintain the happiness that comes with that car, which you will try when you buy the car of your dreams. But finally one day you have to get bored with that car,

"That's why Lord Shri Krishna had said in the Gita that "change is the rule of the world" which is also applicable to our every happiness."

After reading so many thoughts related to the topic of happiness, you must have felt that this author writes his book in a state of intoxication, which is also an expert in diverting from the issue. But this is not the case at all, because the way dust remains on top of an ark is hidden in every secret. Before you open the ark, you have to face and clean that dust, similarly, before knowing the secret of every artist, you have to deal with the dust of useful ideas accumulated on it, Only then will you be able to digest the next secret even better.

Tik-Tik 1, Tik-Tik 2, Tik-Tik 3, that is the secret,

but again there is a twist in it which is that you have to feel a sad situation in your heart and mind before knowing that secret. You have to think about that situation in such a way that you are present in that situation now, only then you will be able to digest that secret in the right way. Otherwise, you have a wealth of experience with you, in which 100% participation of this situation will be there.

Suppose that you are a better person than many people in the world, that is, you are a successful person. Which inspires everyone. Everyone wants to learn some good things from you, especially those hidden rules, people want to know from you, due to which you are known as the most successful person in your field. It is not that you are a very jealous person who does not want to reveal the reasons for your success to anyone. That too thinking that if other people also come to know that way, then those people can also get the treasure of success like me. Which I don't want. No, your nature is also generous and intelligent like every successful person in this world.

"Generous" means that,

every successful person likes to share his knowledge and experience with everyone hidden behind his success.

"Sensible" means that,

You also know that By you showing the way to success, Not everyone can be successful.

Everyone who wants to be successful, will also have to walk on that path, he will also have to give a lot of time to that path, maybe there will be many problems in the way, which people will have to face.

Many people listen to a successful person, that too because all of them see only the person standing on the top, not the mountain, whose difficulty that person has reached there by climbing. Out of those listeners, a very small number of people apply those rules and lessons to their lives.

Based on these hidden laws of life, you are again invited with great respect (which includes flattery and false prestige) to give a speech on the reasons for your success at a school function. You were very excited about that speech that day, so much so that you did not consider it appropriate to do the routine work done at the beginning of your day. You quickly got ready and went to the school of the children playing and laughing.

As you may have heard from many intelligent people, this thought is said that excess in any work is always harmful. In the same way, you also became a victim of too much haste to reach that school that day. Two hours before the appointed time, you got seated on your flower-adorned chair, which was placed on a stage for your sitting. Where the time stops for someone, these two hours too soon passed and you were called to the mic by a beautiful anchor to give a speech of your success. You grabbed the mic with great enthusiasm and started your speech amidst applause.

Some wise people have also put forth the idea that your sins are always with you and when the occasion comes, they pounce on you. That is, on that day, due to your enthusiasm, you did not carry out the daily tasks that were done at the beginning of your day, its effect was now affecting you. In the middle of your encouraging speech, you started feeling heavy pressure in your stomach. The volume of the words you uttered aloud slowly began to decrease. The speech for which you were very happy since morning while giving the same speech, you started feeling like a person suffering in hell. You hurriedly sat down on your assigned chair, saying "That's just the secret of my success" in the middle of your speech that you were about to run for a long time. All the students of that school and all the teachers were constantly clapping for you. Your cheers were reverberating. Everyone present on the stage with you was praising you for your speech. But since the time the movement started in your stomach, you were free from the trap of this illusion. Now you had nothing to do with this world, just one last time let me enter any toilet of this hypocritical world. Just fulfil this last wish, O Lord. Such taking away from the world thoughts were coming into your mind.

But despite having so many wishes and despite achieving so much of your success, you could not get down from that stage and go to any toilet because of your shame and respect for the school. You were tormented inside for a long time, Which could have been treated by spending your time in a toilet for a few minutes.

Eventually, that hope came, the program placed in your success ended and as soon as it ended, you ran faster than the children, went to one of the children's toilets and gave rest to your age-old desire. Even if someone at that time gave you all the wealth of this world and offered you not to open the door of that toilet in exchange for that money, even then you would have turned down that wealth and decided to spend your whole life in that normal toilet. In this way, you had a passion to be free from the pressure that had come on you. You won your battle and you left that toilet with your beautiful smile.

After reading this example, you must be thinking that how smelly and this example that is not within the limits of any author has been presented, and many people reading it must have been thinking that how can you see this situation by connecting it to the secret of an artist? I do not want to know such a secret whose path passes through a toilet.

You are justified in being angry and creating all kinds of logical thoughts in your mind. I do not want to hurt the love associated with any of your artists in any way. But to understand the depth of that secret, it is necessary for you to feel such a situation with truth, otherwise, the purpose of this chapter will remain in just a few written words.

If you want to recover your money on this book, then let's know the secret which is of every artist.

Let's go again to your fictional story in which you are in that stage in which you have just won the painful battle related to your body by going to that school toilet, And you must know that how much happiness you get on every victory in life. Especially your brain. It doesn't matter to your mind, whether what you have won is important to your life or not. For every small success that is achieved by any activity you do, your brain produces hormones of happiness on that successful outcome. They are called "Dopamine" in scientific language. It is also formed when we achieve something in our life or are free from any kind of trouble or our long-pressed desire is fulfilled.

Like, when you were not getting off the stage even if you wanted, under that painful pressure that came in your stomach. You were not able to see any toilet even if you wanted to. You were fighting with that yearning for a long time and when that cumbersome program came to an end and you ran towards your destination, you quickly opened the door of that toilet and by going inside it you rectified your old sin, that is, The work that you did not do that morning, you did that activity by going to that bathroom. When you had completed that important activity, the happiness you felt on your face at that time, the satisfaction you felt at that time, at that time your brain was attacked by a huge amount of happiness hormones, Instead of this success, you can hardly get a taste of that high level in any other success.

Similarly, when an artist belongs to whatever field when he expresses himself through his art. When he works to fulfil that art with his heart. When doing that art, no other thought comes to his mind. When he is actually what he is while doing that art, that is, he feels himself only when he is doing his art. Every artist gets the same level of relaxation while doing and after doing their art that you achieved through that toilet.

If you want to understand this even better, then you can keep a writer in your mind and ask, how does a writer keep writing without any greed? Now many of you must be thinking that a writer fulfils his greed by selling many of his books. It's not like this. Do books start selling from the beginning of every author? Does every writer start getting people's attention and applause in his early days?

No, the birth of every writer begins with knowing himself. He writes for himself first and whether or not to go further in this art of his own? Keeps searching for this question. When a writer comes to know that true happiness comes from writing. He gets satisfaction from putting his thoughts on paper. When a person sees the purpose of his life in his writing, then a person becomes a writer in the right form. Because coming in this situation, any writer writes from his heart, and the work of the one who writes from the heart is something else.

Suppose, a writer thought of writing his thoughts on some issue. He had been thinking about that issue for a long time. When he started seeing all the aspects related to that issue in his mind, then he started feeling thirsty to write down all the thoughts related to that issue. How long had he been yearning to write? He wanted to narrate all the thoughts roaming in his mind, and when he got that opportunity, he completely emptied his mind of those thoughts by writing down everything that was going on in his mind. When he finished writing, the peace he found at that time, The happiness that he felt in that moment and most importantly during and after writing that issue which he felt in the true sense of himself. He cannot get what he gets from writing, from any work in this world and any other dimension of success. This is the thing he would have come to know during his writing activities.

That's why every artist is so happy while doing his work. That is why every artist, even if he does not get the right value for his art, still keeps on doing that art. No matter how many taunts and bad things his family, relatives, neighbours and friends keep talking to him, yet he does not feel like doing any other subject than doing that art, and the artist who does every art from his heart, Not because of anyone's saying or greed, that artist becomes successful in his life. It is a different matter that it may take some time to achieve that success, but the day the lovers of real art see that art, from that day the drums of that art will play everywhere.

Secret Two

Always an artist tells only those things through the medium of his art, which his people usually do not pay attention to. The attention that the artist should have got, he is not getting that much attention as a common person by the people around him. Therefore, every artist creates such a special medium through his art in the form of his art, in which he can easily put his point in front of the people and people become curious to listen to that thing, start giving their importance, and Most importantly, those people who generally did not want to listen to that artist, now they start giving their precious time to listen to that person in the form of his art.

You must have seen many such artists who are not so happy in their personal life because of the person to whom they wanted to say everything, now that person is not with them but it does not mean that they should stop expressing themselves. It is not so, he chose his art and through it created such a magnet, towards which everyone gets pulled. Perhaps that person must have also come who had gone from his life earlier.

Secret Three

What is the secret that every artist makes the ordinary thing, emotion, aspect and any action present in ordinary life so creative and attention-grabbing medium? Because every artist sees everything which is normal for you, that artist does not see it as normal. He keeps trying to make something creative out of that ordinary thing. He doesn't always see life as it is. As you always try to live life on the upper level, which is adopted by every animal in the world. Which means eating, sleeping and running throughout the day to fulfil all the needs of the body. The only difference between you and animals is that you do all these things in a better way. Just like animals sleep on the ground and you make a comfortable sleeping bed based on your financial ability to sleep. Just like animals eat any food dropped on the ground or hunt any small animal which is less capable than them and you eat your favourite food by cooking it. And how do you meet the rest of the needs? And how do animals fulfil their needs? You would know this.

That's why an artist does not see life as it is. He tries to know them inside of every aspect present in life, keeps looking for it and through his artistic ideas, that artist presents to the world in a new form what you would have seen normally, and you Applauding as spectators, and again asking the same question as to how this person does this.

THIRTY-TWO

HOW DO YOU EXPRESS YOURSELF?

You just can't stop expressing yourself. You are not able to control it. Like one day you have decided that from today till the rest of my life I swear that I will not express myself in front of anyone. You think your vow is strong, you are strong. You think that you cannot beat yourself in your game which you have created for yourself that from today onwards I am never expressing anything to anyone. That's not possible at all.

Because everyone needs to express themselves. Because living life without doing this action is like you are tied in some dungeon where there is no one except you and no one comes to meet you.

If you stop expressing yourself, you will never be able to live independently, you will not be able to think properly for any work, you will probably take pills to relieve depression because by keeping this oath, you can go into a deep depression. Because there is always some discomfort inside you which you need to express yourself to overcome. Without it, neither there will be any solution to that discomfort nor discomfort will come out of you.

- And the most important thing is, What if you do not express yourself at all, then you will not be able to enjoy our life to the fullest.

Everyone wants to express themselves, but is "speaking up" the only last option you can express yourself?

Why did you only recommend this form of expressing yourself? it's not necessary. Or is it the rule that everyone has only one medium to express his point of view?

If you want to express yourself on anything, then you have only the option to speak so that people around you can listen to you at that time. If you do not adopt this option, then you will not be counted in that number in which many people have expressed themselves. And you don't have any other option than this. It is not so at all.

It's not necessary. Whether you believe it or not, you want it or not. No one cares about you and your kind wishes. Each person expresses himself through different mediums.

- Just as a person wants to express something, he can choose the medium of speech,
- If one is not comfortable speaking, one can choose to write,
- If someone does not like to write then he can express himself by shouting at his loved ones or his office colleague.
- If someone has too many things to express he can slap a person or fight with someone to express his anger which he held inside for a long time and now he has the opportunity has come to express his anger in such a form as what we call wrong.
- If someone wants to try a new medium of expression, one can laugh very loudly.
- One can use it to express the option of crying. Through this, he becomes free for some time from any anxiety that was lingering in his mind for a long time.

After reading all these options of express you say that if a person does not use any of these options in life to express himself, then what?

So my answer is that it is not possible because if a person is not using any form which is mentioned above then there is a strong possibility that he will have a best friend who will listen to him all. Which would have helped to lighten his heart.

- Perhaps these people would be sharing their words in a secluded place away from the presence of the world.
- Or he may be writing on some paper what he wants to express.

But he or she feels that someone will not understand their words, so he or she decided that they have to keep their words away from people and thought of writing their thoughts in a notebook. So after reading this chapter we concluded that everyone has to express and the form of expression can be changed on different people's mood but whatever medium a person expresses oneself is not important It's important to just express.

Part Seven: Learn to respect book writers

Lastly, also know what is the best way to give feedback to this book and all the books that will come into your life.

THIRTY-THREE
HOW TO GIVE FEEDBACK?

Definition :

First of all, you have to know its exact meaning before going through its process because if you don't know its exact meaning then how can you expect yourself to give a correct response about any product or service.

In general, feedback means reviewing something, analyzing something, giving your thoughts about something. What you feel about something. For example, you bought a book from the market or from any online place to read the subject of your desire. After finishing that book you will now have one or more ideas that you got from the experience of reading that book.

- Meaning that what things in that book do you like good and what things do you like bad about it,
- What was the writing style of the author of that book,
- And the most important question is, did you get satisfaction in the subject you wanted to know about?

Overall it is such that you have conducted an exam for that book and after reading that book you are ready to declare the report card that you have created for that book.

If you give your feedback in this way,

For any product or service then it is called authentic feedback. Because with this kind of process, you give your feedback by not being influenced by anyone's talk, rumours or any person. Like that book that you have bought and someone already told you something bad about that book and also you blindly accepted that person's review. You also tried not to know on what basis that person has given such a review.

- Has that person even read that book or not?
- If he hasn't read that book, then on what basis are you relying on that person's review.

I am not saying that every review available on various products is fake. But if someone does not experience that product, does not use that product and still keeps his thoughts just by looking at that product, whether his thoughts are bad for that product or good, you can not say it is an authentic review. This is not the correct style of giving a review.

So the right process to respond to anything is simple. Just experience that product and service or trust someone else only if they have used that product and service in a real way, if not, then do not follow that person blindly.

> *"Because a bad review of yours can reduce 100 customers of that product or service while that product or service may be good in the true sense."*

> *"And a good review of yours can harm customers who are going to buy a product or service that is not really worth buying by trusting your review."*